Frequently Asked Questions About Response to Intervention

This book is dedicated to my wife, Jackie, and my two children, Jacqueline and Scott, who provide me with the love and purpose for undertaking projects that I hope will enhance the lives of others. My life has been blessed by their loving presence.

I also dedicate this book to my parents, who provided me with the secure and loving foundation from which to grow; my sister, Carol, who makes me smile and laugh; and my brother-in-law, George, who has always been a positive guiding light in my professional journey.

—Roger Pierangelo

This book is dedicated to my wife, Anita, and two children, Collin and Brittany, who give me the greatest life imaginable. The long hours and many years it took to finish this book would never have been possible without the support of my loving wife. Her constant encouragement, understanding, and love provide me with the strength I need to accomplish my goals. I thank her with all my heart. I also dedicate this book to my parents, who have given me support and guidance throughout my life. Their words of encouragement and guidance have made my professional journey a rewarding and successful experience.

—George Giuliani

A STEP-BY-STEP GUIDE FOR EDUCATORS

Frequently Asked Questions About Response to Intervention

ROGER PIERANGELO ~ GEORGE GIULIANI

CORWIN PRESS
A SAGE Company
Thousand Oaks, CA 91320

For information:

Corwin Press
A SAGE Company
2455 Teller Road
Thousand Oaks, California 91320
www.corwinpress.com

SAGE India Pvt. Ltd.
B 1/I 1 Mohan Cooperative
   Industrial Area
Mathura Road, New Delhi 110 044
India

SAGE Ltd.
1 Oliver's Yard
55 City Road
London, EC1Y 1SP
United Kingdom

SAGE Asia-Pacific Pte. Ltd.
33 Pekin Street #02-01
Far East Square
Singapore 048763

Printed in the United States of America

Library of Congress Cataloging-in-Publication Data

Pierangelo, Roger.
Frequently asked questions about response to intervention: a step-by-step guide for educators / Roger Pierangelo, George Giuliani.
    p. cm.
Includes bibliographical references and index.
ISBN 978-1-4129-5428-0 (cloth) — ISBN 978-1-4129-1789-6 (pbk.)
    1. Remedial teaching. 2. Learning disabled children—Education. I. Giuliani, George A., 1938- II. Title.

LB1029 R4P54 2008
371.9—dc22   2007040305

This book is printed on acid-free paper.

07   08   09   10   11   10 9 8 7 6 5 4 3 2 1

Acquisitions Editor:	Allyason Sharp
Managing Editor:	David Chao
Editorial Assistants:	David Gray, Mary Dang
Production Editor:	Appingo Publishing Services
Cover Designer:	Michael Dubowe
Graphic Designer:	Lisa Riley

Contents

Preface

Every day, educators make decisions about children that are of lifelong importance. Among the most profound of these is the conclusion that a child's educational struggles are the result of a disability. Educators engage in this difficult task because they know that, despite the dangers inherent in labeling students, important benefits may follow. When the decision is accurate, it can help parents and children understand the source of difficulties. It opens the door to resources, assistance, and accommodations.

Deciding a child does not have a disability is equally important. That conclusion says to general educators that they can effectively educate the student. It tells parents and students that success is attainable through hard work, practice, and engaged instruction, without special education services.

It is critical that schools make these decisions based on the best information possible. For the majority of children in special education, those identified as having a learning disability (LD), this decision has been made in a climate of uncertainty. For decades the field of learning disabilities has struggled with identification issues both in practice and in the law. However, with the 2004 reauthorization of the Individuals with Disabilities Education Act (IDEA 2004), the climate is changing.

When IDEA was reauthorized in 1997, the U.S. Department of Education Office of Special Education Programs (OSEP) began a process to "carefully review research findings, expert opinion, and practical knowledge...to determine whether changes should be proposed to the procedures for evaluating children suspected of having a specific learning disability" (U.S. Office of Education, 1999, p. 12541).

This review resulted in a "Learning Disabilities Summit." At this summit, a series of papers presented relevant developments in the LD field and provided empirical validation for the use of alternatives to traditional discrepancy models. Following the summit, a series of meetings was conducted to gain consensus in the field regarding issues around LDs. The following are consensus statements from the 2002 Learning Disabilities Roundtable report that apply to LD identification and were influential in the 2004 reauthorization process:

- Identification should include a student-centered, comprehensive evaluation and problem-solving approach that ensures students who have a specific learning disability (SLD) are efficiently identified.

- Decisions regarding eligibility for special education services must draw from information collected from a comprehensive individual evaluation using multiple methods and sources of relevant information.

- Decisions on eligibility must be made through an interdisciplinary team, using informed clinical judgment, directed by relevant data, and based on student needs and strengths.

- The ability-achievement discrepancy formula should not be used for determining eligibility.

- Regular education must assume active responsibility for delivery of high-quality instruction, research-based interventions, and prompt identification of individuals at risk while collaborating with special education and related services personnel.

- Based on an individualized evaluation and continuous progress monitoring, a student who has been identified as having an SLD may need different levels of special education and related services under IDEA at various times during the school experience.

IDEA 2004 represents consensus on at least three points regarding LD identification. These points are (a) the field should move away from the use of aptitude achievement discrepancy models, (b) there needs to be rapid development of alternative methods of identifying students with learning disabilities, and (c) response to intervention (RTI) model is the most credible available method to replace discrepancy. RTI systematizes the clinical judgment, problem solving, and general education interventions recommended in the consensus statements just mentioned. In RTI, students are provided with carefully designed interventions that are research based, and their response to those interventions is carefully tracked. This information is analyzed and used as one component in determining whether a child has a learning disability.

IDEA 2004 includes two important innovations designed to promote change:

1. States may not require school districts to use a severe discrepancy formula in eligibility determination.

2. Districts may use an alternative process including an RTI method described in IDEA 2004 as part of eligibility decisions.

Whatever model the district uses to implement RTI, such an adoption will affect more than a district's special education and evaluation departments. RTI requires a *way of thinking* about instruction, academic achievement, and individual differences that makes it impossible to implement without fully involving general education.

Acknowledgments

In the course of writing this book, we have encountered many outstanding professional sites. Those resources have contributed and continue to contribute enormous information, support, guidance, and education to parents, students, and professionals in the area of special education. Although we have accessed many worthwhile sites, we especially thank and acknowledge the following outstanding sources of information that provide comprehensive sources on the topic of RTI for the public:

- Colorado Department of Education
- Dr. Terry Bergeson and the Special Education, Office of Superintendent of Public Instruction, in the State of Washington
- E. Johnson, D. F. Mellard, D. Fuchs, and M. A. McKnight (2006) and the entire staff at the National Research Center on Learning Disabilities
- New Mexico Public Education Department
- Oregon Department of Education: Office of Student Learning and Partnerships
- U.S. Department of Education: Office of Special Education Programs
- West Virginia Department of Education: Division of Instructional Services

Both Dr. Pierangelo and Dr. Giuliani extend sincere thanks to Allyson Sharp, Mary Dang, and Laureen Shea for all of their hard work and dedication toward making this book a reality. We could not have completed it without your constant support and encouragement

I (Roger Pierangelo) extend thanks to the following: the faculty, administration, and staff of the Department of Graduate Special Education and Literacy at Long Island University; Ollie Simmons, for her friendship, loyalty, and great personality; the students and parents of the Herricks Public Schools I have worked with and known over the past thirty-five years; the late Bill Smyth, a truly gifted and "extraordinary ordinary" man; and Helen Firestone, for her influence on my career and her tireless support of me.

I (George Giuliani) extend sincere thanks to all of my colleagues at Hofstra University in the School of Education and Allied Human Services. I am especially grateful to those who have made my transition to Hofstra University such a smooth one, including Maureen Murphy (dean), Daniel Sciarra (chairperson), Frank Bowe, Diane Schwartz (graduate program director of early childhood special education), Darra Pace, Gloria Wilson, Laurie Johnson, Joan Bloomgarden, Jamie Mitus, Estelle Gellman, Joseph Lechowicz, Holly Seirup, Adele Piombino, Marjorie Butler, Eve Byrne, and Linda Cappa. I also thank my brother and sister, Roger and Claudia; mother-in-law, Ursula Jenkeleit; sisters-in-law, Karen and Cindy; and brothers-in-law, Robert and Bob. They have provided me with encouragement and reinforcement in all of my personal and professional endeavors.

Corwin Press would also like to thank the following reviewers for their significant contributions:

Barbara J Trussell
SPED Para
Harrison High School
Colorado Springs, CO

Joshua Nichols
Building Special Education Supervisor
Mountain Vista Community School
Colorado Springs, CO

Suzanne VanDinter
Special Education Teacher K–5
Wildflower Elementary
Colorado Springs, CO

About the Authors

Roger Pierangelo, PhD, is an associate professor in the Department of Special Education and Literacy at Long Island University. He has been an administrator of special education programs, served for eighteen years as a permanent member of Committees on Special Education, has over thirty years of experience in the public school system as a general education classroom teacher and school psychologist, and serves as a consultant to numerous private and public schools, PTA, and SEPTA groups. Dr. Pierangelo has also been an evaluator for the New York State Office of Vocational and Rehabilitative Services and a director of a private clinic. He is a New York State–licensed clinical psychologist, a certified school psychologist, and a Board Certified Diplomate Fellow in Student and Adolescent Psychology and Forensic Psychology. Dr. Pierangelo is the executive director of the National Association of Special Education Teachers (NASET) and an executive director of the American Academy of Special Education Professionals (AASEP). He also holds the office of vice president of the National Association of Parents with Children in Special Education (NAPCSE).

Dr. Pierangelo earned his BS from St. John's University, MS from Queens College, Professional Diploma from Queens College, PhD from Yeshiva University, and Diplomate Fellow in Student and Adolescent Psychology and Forensic Psychology from the International College of Professional Psychology. He is a member of the American Psychological Association, New York State Psychological Association, Nassau County Psychological Association, New York State Union of Teachers, and Phi Delta Kappa.

Dr. Pierangelo is the author of multiple books by Corwin Press, including *The Big Book of Special Education Resources* and *The Step-by-Step Series for Special Educators.*

George Giuliani, JD, PsyD, is a full-time tenured associate professor and the director of Special Education at Hofstra University's School of Education and Allied Human Services in the Department of Counseling, Research, Special Education, and Rehabilitation. Dr. Giuliani earned his BA from the College of the Holy Cross, MS from St. John's University, JD from City University Law School, and PsyD from Rutgers University, the Graduate School of Applied and Professional Psychology. He earned Board Certification as a Diplomate Fellow in Student and Adolescent Psychology and Forensic Psychology from the

International College of Professional Psychology. He is also a New York State–licensed psychologist and certified school psychologist and has an extensive private practice focusing on students with special needs. He is a member of the American Psychological Association, New York State Psychological Association, National Association of School Psychologists, Suffolk County Psychological Association, Psi Chi, American Association of University Professors, and the Council for Exceptional Students.

Dr. Giuliani is the president of the National Association of Parents with Children in Special Education (NAPCSE), executive director of the National Association of Special Education Teachers (NASET), and executive director of the American Academy of Special Education Professionals (AASEP). He is a consultant for school districts and early childhood agencies and has provided numerous workshops for parents and guardians and teachers on a variety of special education and psychological topics. He is the coauthor of numerous books by Corwin Press, including *The Big Book of Special Education Resources* and *The Step-by-Step Series for Special Educators*.

Step I

Making Sense of the Basic Principles of RTI

Question #1: What Is Response to Intervention (RTI)?

The Response to Intervention (RTI) process is a multitiered approach to providing services and interventions to struggling learners at increasing levels of intensity. RTI can be used for making decisions about general, compensatory, and special education, creating a well-integrated and seamless system of instruction and intervention guided by child outcome data. RTI calls for early identification of learning and behavioral needs; close collaboration among teachers, special education personnel, and parents; and a systemic commitment to locating and employing the necessary resources to ensure that students make progress in the general education curriculum. RTI is an initiative that takes place in the general education environment.

The National Research Center on Learning Disabilities (NRCLD, 2006) has defined RTI as "an assessment and intervention process for systematically monitoring student progress and making decisions about the need for instructional modifications or increasingly intensified services using progress monitoring data."

RTI is an integrated approach to service delivery that encompasses general, remedial, and special education through a multitiered service-delivery model. It utilizes a problem-solving framework to identify and address academic and behavioral difficulties for all students using scientific, research-based instruction. Essentially, RTI is the practice of (a) providing high-quality instruction/intervention matched to all students needs and (b) using learning rate over time and level of performance to (c) make important educational decisions to guide instruction (National Association of State Directors of Special Education [NASDSE], 2005). RTI practices are proactive, incorporating both prevention and intervention, and they are effective at all levels from early childhood through high school.

Question #2: What Is the Purpose of RTI?

RTI is intended to reduce the incidence of "instructional casualties" by ensuring that students are provided high-quality instruction with fidelity. By using RTI, districts can provide interventions to students as soon as a need arises. This is very different, for example, from the methods associated with the aptitude-achievement discrepancy models traditionally utilized for specific learning disability (SLD) identification, which have been criticized as a "wait to fail" approach.

The Individuals with Disabilities Education Improvement Act (IDEA) of 2004 allows the use of a student's "response to scientific, research-based intervention" (§1414 (B)(6)(A)) as part of an evaluation. RTI functions as an alternative for learning disability (LD) evaluations within the general evaluation requirements of IDEA 2004. The statute continues to include requirements that apply to all undisability categories, such as the use of validated, unbiased methods and evaluation in all suspected areas of difficulty. IDEA 2004 adds a new concept in eligibility that prohibits children from being found eligible for special education if they have not received instruction in reading that includes the five essential components of reading instruction identified by the Reading First Program. These requirements are those recognized by the National Reading Panel: phonemic awareness, phonics, reading fluency (including oral reading skills), vocabulary development, and reading comprehension strategies. RTI is included under this general umbrella. By using RTI, it is possible to identify students early, reduce referral bias, and test various theories for why a child is failing. It was included in the law specifically to offer an alternative to discrepancy models.

A key element of an RTI approach is the provision of early intervention when students first experience academic difficulties, with the goal of improving the achievement of all students, including those who may have an LD. In addition to the preventive and remedial services this approach may provide to at-risk students, it shows promise for contributing data useful for identifying LDs. Thus, a student exhibiting (a) significantly low achievement and (b) insufficient RTI may be regarded as being at risk for an LD and, in turn, as possibly in need of special education and related services. The assumption behind this paradigm, which has been referred to as a dual discrepancy (L. S. Fuchs, D. Fuchs, & Speece, 2002, is that when provided with quality instruction and remedial services, a student without disabilities will make satisfactory progress.

The concept of RTI has always been the focus of the teaching/learning process and a basic component of accountability in general education: In other words, does instruction (i.e., strategies, methods, interventions, or curriculum) lead to increased learning and appropriate progress? In the past few years, RTI has taken on a more specific connotation, especially in IDEA 2004, as an approach to remedial intervention that also generates data to inform instruction and identify students who may require special education and related services. Today, many educators, researchers, and other professionals are exploring the usefulness of an RTI approach as an alternative that can provide (a) data for more effective and earlier identification of students with LD and (b) a systematic way to ensure that students experiencing educational difficulties receive more timely and effective support (Gresham, 2002; Learning Disabilities Roundtable, 2002, 2005; National Research Council, 2002; President's Commission on Excellence in Special Education, 2002).

Question #3: Why Is RTI Important?

According to current early reading research, all except a very few children can become competent readers by the end of the third grade. RTI is a process that provides immediate intervention to struggling students at the first indication of failure to learn. Through systematic screening of all students in the early grades, classroom teachers identify those who are not mastering critical reading skills and provide differentiated intervention to small groups of students. Continuous progress monitoring of students' responses to those interventions allows teachers to identify students in need of additional intervention and to adjust instruction accordingly.

Response to Intervention is about building better readers in the early grades and consists of multitiered reading instruction in the general education classroom. In an RTI model, *all* students receive high-quality reading instruction and struggling readers receive additional and increasingly more intense intervention. Early intervention and prevention of reading difficulties are fundamental to the process. However, if a student's learning history and classroom performance warrant intervention, a multidisciplinary team may determine that the student has a disability and needs special education services to ensure continued and appropriate academic progress.

Three major developments concerning the education of students with learning problems have coalesced to establish RTI as a promising approach. First, long-standing concerns about the inadequacies of the ability-achievement discrepancy criterion—which was a component of the Individuals with Disabilities Education Act of 1997 for identifying LDs—have accentuated the need to develop alternative mechanisms for the identification of LDs. At the LD Summit of August 2001, sponsored by the Office of Special Education Programs, RTI was the alternative proposed by several researchers (e.g., Gresham, 2002; Marston, 2001).

Second, special education has been used to serve struggling learners who do not have LDs or other disabilities. An RTI approach has been suggested as a way to reduce referrals to special education by providing well-designed instruction and intensified interventions in general education, thereby distinguishing between students who perform poorly in school due to factors such as inadequate prior instruction and students with LDs who need more intensive and specialized instruction.

A third major reason for the increased interest in an RTI approach has been the abundance of recent research on reading difficulties, in particular, the national network of research studies coordinated by the National Institute of Child Health and Human Development (NICHD). A number of NICHD research studies have demonstrated that well-designed instructional programs or approaches result in significant improvements for the majority of students with early reading.

Question #4: What Are Other Benefits of RTI?

An RTI approach, with its focus on student outcomes, may increase accountability for all learners within general education, whether or not they are eventually referred for special education and related services. An RTI approach promotes collaboration and shared responsibility among general educators, special educators, teachers of English language learners, related service personnel, administrators, and parents.

In addition to these general education benefits, proponents of an RTI approach cite several other potential benefits:

1. Earlier identification of students by means of a problem-solving approach rather than by an ability-achievement discrepancy formula. An RTI approach has the potential to eliminate the "wait to fail" situation that occurs when an ability-achievement discrepancy formula is used to determine whether a student qualifies as having an LD. When a psychometric formula is used to establish the discrepancy criterion, it is difficult to identify students as having an LD until at least the third grade. Under an RTI approach, students may receive specialized interventions at a much earlier point in their schooling, and considerably in advance of any determination of special education eligibility (Vaughn & Fuchs, 2003).

2. Reduction in the number of students referred for special education and related services. One goal of an RTI approach is to distinguish students whose achievement problems are due to LDs or other disabilities that require special education and related services from the larger group of students with achievement problems due to other causes. By providing appropriate instruction for students at risk, as well as for those with LDs, an RTI approach has the potential to reduce the number of students referred for special education and related services (see Deno, Grimes, Reschly, & Schrag, 2001; Ikeda & Gustafson, 2002; Tilly, Grimes, & Reschly, 1993.

3. Reduction in the overidentification of minority students. The RTI approach shows promise for reducing bias in the assessment of students from culturally and linguistically diverse backgrounds, and for providing a positive impact on the disproportionate placement of African American students in special education. When an RTI was used over a four-year period in the

Minneapolis Public Schools, Marston, Muyskens, Lau, and Canter (2003) noted a reduction in both the number of African American students referred for evaluation and the number placed in special education. Attention to and concern about possible bias is reflected in IDEA 2004, which requires states not only to keep track of how many minority students are being identified for special education, but also to provide "comprehensive, coordinated, early-intervention programs" for students in groups that are determined to be overrepresented.

4. Provision of more instructionally relevant data than traditional methods of identification. An RTI approach emphasizes progress monitoring through the use of curriculum-based or classroom-based assessment, student portfolios, teacher observations, and criterion-referenced standard achievement measures. Thus, if a child is eventually identified as having an LD, instructionally relevant information, whether it indicates what did not work or what has not yet been tried, will be available to guide the team in developing the student's individualized education program (IEP).

Question #5: Is RTI a "New Approach"?

RTI is not a new approach. It is recognizable under other names such as *dynamic assessment, diagnostic teaching,* and *precision teaching*. Those terms, however, have been applied to approaches used to maximize student progress through sensitive measurement of the effects of instruction. RTI applies similar methods to draw conclusions and make LD classification decisions about students. The underlying assumption is that using RTI will identify children whose intrinsic difficulties make them the most difficult to teach. Engaging a student in a dynamic process like RTI provides an opportunity to assess various hypotheses about the causes of a child's difficulties, such as motivation or constitutional factors like attention.

Question #6: When Did RTI Become "Law"?

At the core of No Child Left Behind (NCLB), passed in 2001, is the goal that all children have the opportunity to achieve in school. The law emphasizes the importance of well-prepared professionals, evidence-based practice, and accountability. In 2004, the reauthorization of IDEA 2004 aligned with NCLB and changed the landscape of identification and service delivery for students with disabilities.

On December 3, 2004, Congress reauthorized the Individuals with Disabilities Education Improvement Act (2004). The language that Congress uses in IDEA 2004 and No Child Left Behind (2001) stresses the use of professionally sound interventions and instruction based on defensible research, as well as the delivery of effective academic and behavior programs to improve student performance. Congress believes that as a result, fewer children will require special education services. Provisions of IDEA 2004 allow school districts to use scientific, research-based interventions as an alternative method for identifying students with specific learning disabilities (SLDs). This process is generally referred to as Response to Intervention (RTI).

Of particular relevance to the process of SLD determination are the following provisions of the statute:

- Local educational agencies (LEAs) shall not be required to take into consideration whether a child has a severe discrepancy between achievement and intellectual ability (IDEA, 2004).
- LEAs may consider a student's response to science-based instruction.
- Response to Intervention (RTI) is not specifically identified in the law.
- LEAs are given flexibility in determining SLD implementation options.
- Using special education funding to provide early intervening services for all students is permitted.

Ultimately, IDEA 2004 addresses the use of RTI in two respects. First, it allows for the use of RTI data as part of an evaluation for special education to assist in the identification and determination of eligibility of students with LDs, conceivably as an alternative to use of the ability-achievement discrepancy criterion. Second, it creates the option of using up to 15 percent of Part B funds for "early intervening services…for students…who have not been identified as needing special education or related services but who need additional academic and behavioral support to succeed in a general education environment." (Lemon, 2005, p.1)

Question #7: Why Was There a Movement for a Change Toward RTI?

This movement toward change stems from criticisms of current SLD determination components, procedures, and criteria. These criticisms include irrelevance of aptitude-achievement discrepancy and cognitive measures to instructional planning or outcomes, lack of equitable treatment across educational settings, and delays in disability determination. Another criticism of practices has been that students were judged to have an SLD without an assessment of the availability and use of general education interventions that have proven their effectiveness for students presenting similar behaviors of concern (e.g., limited reading acquisition). One could not be confident that the achievement and behavior problems that a child presented were inherent to the child or attributable to shortcomings in the instructional settings.

Earlier statutes regarding the determination of SLDs included a provision for evaluating the extent to which students had received appropriate learning experiences. However, no systematic process was outlined in the earlier regulations for ensuring that the learning experiences provided before referral for evaluation were those that have been found to be typically effective for the child's age and ability levels. The responsiveness to science-based intervention concept in IDEA 2004 is an elaboration or greater specification of this basic concept. With this emphasis, school staffs may consider how a student's performance in general education and, more specifically, the student's performance in response to specific scientific, research-based instruction, informs SLD determination.

Question #8: What Are the Core Principles of RTI?

RTI is comprised of seven core principles that represent recommended RTI practices (Mellard, 2003). These principles represent systems that must be in place to ensure effective implementation of RTI systems and establish a framework to guide and define the practice.

1. **Use all available resources to teach all students.** RTI practices are built on the belief that all students can learn. One of the biggest changes associated with RTI is that it requires educators to shift their thinking from the student to the intervention. This means that the initial evaluation no longer focuses on "what is wrong with the student." Instead, there is a shift to an

examination of the curricular, instructional, and environmental variables that change inadequate learning progress. Once the correct set of intervention variables has been identified, schools must then provide the means and systems for delivering resources so that effective teaching and learning can occur. In doing so, schools must provide resources in a manner that is directly proportional to students' needs. This will require districts and schools to reconsider current resource allocation systems so that financial and other support structures for RTI practices can be established and sustained.

2. **Use scientific, research-based interventions/instruction.** The critical element of RTI systems is the delivery of scientific, research-based interventions with fidelity in general, remedial, and special education. This means that the curriculum and instructional approaches must have a high probability of success for the majority of students. By using research-based practices, schools efficiently use time and resources and protect students from ineffective instructional and evaluative practices. Since instructional practices vary in efficacy, ensuring that the practices and curriculum have demonstrated validity is an important consideration in the selection of interventions. With the absence of definitive research, schools should implement promising practices, monitor the effectiveness, and modify implementation based on the results.

3. **Monitor classroom performance.** General education teachers play a vital role in designing and providing high-quality instruction. Furthermore, they are in the best position to assess students' performance and progress against grade-level standards in the general education curriculum. This principle emphasizes the importance of general education teachers in monitoring student progress rather than waiting to determine how students are learning in relation to their same-age peers based on results of statewide or districtwide assessments.

4. **Conduct universal screening/benchmarking.** School staff conduct universal screening in all core academic areas and in behavior. Screening data on all students can provide an indication of an individual student's performance and progress compared to the peer group's performance and progress. These data form the basis for an initial examination of individual and group patterns on specific academic skills (e.g., identifying letters of the alphabet or reading a list of high-frequency words) as well as behavior skills (e.g., attendance, cooperation, tardiness,

truancy, suspensions, and/or disciplinary actions). Universal screening is the least intensive level of assessment completed within an RTI system and helps educators and parents identify students early who might be "at risk." Since screening data may not be as reliable as other assessments, it is important to use multiple sources of evidence in reaching inferences regarding students "at risk."

5. **Use a multitier model of service delivery.** An RTI approach incorporates a multitiered model of service delivery in which each tier represents an increasingly intense level of services associated with increasing levels of learner needs. The system described in this manual reflects a three-tiered design. All multitiered systems, regardless of the number of levels chosen, should yield the same practical effects and outcomes.

    In an RTI system, all students receive instruction in the core curriculum supported by strategic and intensive interventions when needed. Therefore, all students, including those with disabilities, are found in Tiers 1, 2, and 3. Important features such as universal screening, progress monitoring, fidelity of implementation, and problem solving occur within each tier. The basic tiered model reflects what we know about students in school: their instructional needs will vary. Thus, the nature of the academic or behavioral intervention changes at each tier, becoming more rigorous as the student moves through the tiers.

    Tier 1 represents the largest group of students—approximately 80–90 percent—who are performing adequately within the core curriculum. Tier 2 comprises a smaller group of students, typically 5–10 percent of the student population. These students will need strategic interventions to raise their achievement to proficiency or above based on a lack of Response to Interventions at Tier 1. Tier 3 contains the fewest number of students, usually 1–5 percent. These students will need intensive interventions if their learning is to be appropriately supported,

6. **Make data-based decisions.** Within an RTI system, teams use problem solving and/or standard treatment protocol techniques to make decisions. The purpose of these teams is to find the best instructional approach for a student with an academic or behavioral problem. Problem solving and standard treatment protocol decision making provide a structure for using data to monitor student learning so that good decisions

can be made at each tier with a high probability of success. When using the problem-solving method, teams answer four interrelated questions: (a) Is there a problem and what is it? (b) Why is it happening? (c) What are we going to do about it? (d) Did our interventions work? (NASDSE, 2005). Problem solving and standard treatment protocol techniques ensure that decisions about a student's needs are driven by the student's response to high-quality interventions.

7. **Monitor progress frequently.** In order to determine if the intervention is working for a student, the decision-making team must establish and implement progress monitoring. Progress monitoring is the use of assessments that can be collected frequently and are sensitive to small changes in student behavior. Data collected through progress monitoring will inform the decision-making team whether changes in the instruction or goals are needed. Informed decisions about students' needs require frequent data collection to provide reliable measures of progress. Various curriculum-based measurements are useful tools for monitoring students' progress.

Question #9: What Is a Tiered Service-Delivery Model?

As noted earlier, an RTI approach incorporates a multitiered system of service delivery in which each tier represents an increasingly intense level of services. Students move fluidly from tier to tier. A multitiered concept aligns all available resources to support and address students' needs regardless of their eligibility for other programs. It is important to note that RTI is not a placement model; it is a flexible service model.

Question #10: What Is the Three-Tier Model?

The Three-Tier model is a prevention model intended to identify students before they fail and to provide the supports students need to learn essential academic and behavioral skills. Research demonstrates that waiting for students to "catch on" or "catch up" does not lead to higher student achievement. Students need explicit, targeted instruction and intervention to succeed.

Question #11: What Is the Focus of Tier 1?

Tier 1 is designed to meet the needs of a majority of the school population and has three critical elements:

1. A research-based core curriculum

2. Short-cycle assessments for all students at least three times a year to determine their instructional needs

3. Sustained professional development to equip teachers with tools necessary for effectively teaching content area

In Tier 1, the goal is to prevent failure and optimize learning by offering the most effective instruction possible to the greatest number of students. Instruction takes place in a regular education setting and is, for the most part, whole class (scientifically based) instruction that produces good results for most students. Based on data, classroom teachers monitor student progress and differentiate instruction for students who do not meet grade-level expectations.

Question #12: What Is the Focus of Tier 2?

Tier 2 is for students who are falling behind same-age peers and need additional, targeted interventions to meet grade-level expectations. In Tier 2, the goal is to accelerate learning for students who need more intensive support. In Tier 2, the interventions typically take place in a regular setting and may include instruction to small groups of students, targeted interventions, and frequent progress monitoring.

Question #13: What Is the Focus of Tier 3?

Tier 3 is designed for students who still have considerable difficulty in mastering necessary academic and/or behavioral skills, even after Tier 1 and Tier 2 instruction and interventions. Tier 3 addresses students' needs through intensive individualized services. In Tier 3, students receive intensive and highly focused, intentional, research-based instruction, possibly over a long period of time. Tier 3 involves students who did not respond to Tier 2 intervention. These students undergo a more formal diagnostic evaluation.

Question #14: Does RTI Always Have to Be Three-Tiered?

RTI is a multitiered service-delivery intervention. Much discussion continues surrounding the issues of how many tiers constitute an adequate intervention (O'Connor, Tilly, Vaughn, & Marston, 2003). Although there is no universal RTI model, it is generally understood to include multiple tiers that provide a sequence of programs and services for students showing academic difficulties. Tier 1 provides high-quality instruction and behavioral supports in general education, Tier 2 provides more specialized instruction for students whose performance and rate of progress lag behind classroom peers, and Tier 3 provides comprehensive evaluation by a multidisciplinary team to determine if the student has a disability and is eligible for special education and related services.

Question #15: Is RTI Just Applicable to Special Education?

RTI has application for general education, compensatory education, and special education. Most important, RTI promotes research-based instruction and quality teaching that result in better outcomes for all students.

Question #16: What Are Some Conditions and Activities of RTI?

Ultimately, RTI may include the following conditions and activities:

- High-quality instructional and behavioral supports are in place.
- Scientific, research-based intervention is delivered by qualified personnel with expertise in the intervention used and in the areas of student difficulty.
- Student progress is continuously monitored.
- Data-based documentation is maintained on each student.
- Systematic documentation verifies that interventions are implemented with fidelity, integrity, and the intended intensity.
- Decisions are made by a collaborative team of school staff who review response data and other information required to ensure a comprehensive evaluation.

- Interventions address the individual student's difficulties at the needed level of intensity and with the support of needed resources and personnel.
- A written document describing the specific components and structure of the process to be used is available to parents and professionals.
- Parent notification and involvement are documented.

Question #17: Is There Federal Funding to Support RTI Related Activities?

As a schoolwide prevention approach, RTI includes changing instruction for struggling students to help them improve academic skills and behavior. To meet the needs of all students, the educational system must use its collective resources to intervene early and provide appropriate interventions and supports to prevent learning and behavioral problems from becoming larger issues. To support these efforts, the Individuals with Disabilities Education Improvement Act of 2004 gives more financial flexibility to local education agencies (LEAs). Under the Early Intervening Services (EIS) provisions in the law, to help minimize over identification and unnecessary referrals, LEAs can use up to 15 percent of their federal IDEA funds to provide academic and behavioral services to support prevention and early identification for struggling learners [P.L. 108-446, §613(f) (1)]. LEAs also have greater flexibility to use up to 50 percent of any increases that they receive in federal funding for Title I activities. These funds may be used for professional development of non-special-education staff, as well as for RTI-related activities.

IDEA allows 15 percent of special education funds to be used to provide early intervening services for students who have academic or behavioral difficulties but are not identified as having learning disabilities. A district that has been identified as having significant disproportionality in identifying students for special education is required to provide early intervening services. This new provision is a huge breakthrough for students at risk of having learning disabilities. They now are eligible to receive early intervention services as early as kindergarten and first grade instead of waiting until they experience a prolonged and significant period of academic failure, often as late as third or fourth grade, which is often the case under the IQ-achievement discrepancy model.

Question #18: Does RTI Address Challenging Behavior?

IDEA 2004 discusses the use of RTI in relation to the identification and support for students with possible specific learning disabilities. However, another dimension also stems from the common observation that many students struggle academically and exhibit problem behaviors. Students misbehave for a variety of reasons. Some students misbehave because they "won't do it," or because they try and "can't do it." Regardless, the fact remains that behavior and academic success are closely linked and need to be addressed simultaneously or in a concerted effort.

In an RTI approach to behavior, systematically collected behavioral data (e.g., observations, office referral patterns, ratings, etc.) provide a basis for making decisions on behavior supports. A student who displays challenging behavior should be assessed, just as the student would if an academic concern was raised. Based on the results, staff uses evidence-based practices to support the student in reducing challenging behaviors and developing positive attitudes toward academic and social life. At the highest level of rigor, evidence-based interventions for behavior mean a randomized, controlled trial design, followed by quasi-experimental controlled design (typically denotes nonrandom assignment to condition). Additional evidence of efficacy is indicated by studies with a statistically significant positive effect, which is a positive effect sustained for at least one year post intervention, and replication of the effect in one or more settings and/or populations. Many evidence-based behavioral interventions should be considered, such as methods based on applied behavior analysis (e.g., reinforcement), social learning (e.g., teaching expected behaviors through modeling and role-playing), and cognitive behavioral methods to teach "thinking skills" (e.g., problem solving, impulse control, anger management, etc.).

IDEA 2004 did not change the criteria required to establish an emotional behavioral disorder (EBD). However, an evaluation group may include RTI data when considering whether a student has a disability that meets EBD criteria. The universal screening that applies to behavior at Tier I suggests that schools have effective positive behavioral systems in place. Despite this, there will be some students that will need additional strategic and/or intensive behavioral interventions.

Question #19: Does a School District's "Child Find" Obligations Change Within RTI Systems?

Implementing an RTI system does not alter a school district's obligations to identify students with disabilities ("child find"). Parents, teachers, or anyone else can initiate a referral at any time. Schools need to ensure that staff is trained to refer students who may require special education services no matter their tier level. This means that students do not need to advance through the multitiered system as a condition before a referral is made. In certain circumstances, a student may have progressed through the multiple tiers without any success (e.g., at least two Tier 3 interventions have been unsuccessful). In this situation, a disability should be suspected and a referral must be made. District personnel should be aware that a parent or anyone else has the right to make a special education referral even for students who have not yet demonstrated a lack of responsiveness to an intervention. A district or school may continue RTI interventions if they have already been initiated while processing the referral and determining whether or not the student is a candidate for special education evaluation within required timelines.

Question #20: Is Family Involvement an Important Component for Successful RTI Programs?

Involving family at all phases is a key aspect of a successful RTI program. As members of the decision-making team, parents/guardians can provide a critical perspective on students, thus increasing the likelihood that RTI interventions will be effective. For this reason, schools must make a concerted effort to involve parents as early as possible, beginning with instruction in the core curriculum. This can be done through traditional methods such as parent-teacher conferences, regularly scheduled meetings, or by other methods. This must be done by notifying parents of student progress within the RTI system on a regular basis.

Districts and schools should provide parents with written information about RTI programs and should be prepared to answer questions about RTI processes. The written information should explain how the system is different from a traditional education system and explain the vital and collaborative role that parents play within an RTI system. The more parents are involved as players, the greater the opportunity for successful RTI outcomes.

Because RTI is a method of delivering the general education curriculum for all students, written consent is not required before administering universal screenings, (CBMs), and targeted assessments within a multitiered RTI system when these tools are used to determine instructional need. However, when a student fails to respond to interventions and the decision is made to evaluate a student for special education eligibility, written consent must be obtained in accordance with special education procedures. When developing screening measures, districts should also consider the parallel measures that may be used for evaluation.

Failure to communicate and reach out to parents will lead to confusion, especially among parents who believe that their children have a learning disability. Schools may also want to provide other means for keeping parents engaged and informed, such as the following actions:

- Involving parents in state and local planning for RTI adoption
- Providing parents with written material informing them of their right to refer their child at any time for special education evaluation as stipulated in IDEA 2004
- Providing parents with written material that outlines the criteria for determining eligibility under IDEA 2004 and the role of RTI data in making LD determinations

Taking measures to build strong, productive relationships with parents can only increase the likelihood that students will benefit greatly from an RTI model.

Question #21: Can RTI Promote Optimal Learning?

Optimal learning outcomes occur when students' skills and abilities closely match the curriculum and instruction within the classroom. When a mismatch occurs, student outcomes and learning suffer. Quality classroom instruction usually provides a good match for most students; but for other students, success is not easy. The hypothesis is that with RTI, these struggling students can be identified and provided appropriate instruction early, thus increasing the likelihood that they can be successful and maintain their class placement.

Question #22: What Is Fidelity?

Fidelity refers to the degree to which RTI components are implemented as designed, intended, and planned. Fidelity is achieved through sufficient time allocation, adequate intervention intensity, qualified and trained staff, and sufficient materials and resources. Fidelity is vital in universal screening, instructional delivery and progress monitoring.

Question #23: Does Implementation of RTI Methods Require a Serious Commitment?

Implementation of RTI methods occurs within the general education environment and requires a serious schoolwide commitment. All school staff and parents play vital roles in an RTI approach. A successful RTI system requires the commitment of many people including, parents, teachers, specialists, administrators, and paraeducators. It requires that all work cooperatively in supporting each student as he or she progresses.

Data management is also crucial within an RTI system. Schools that use RTI will need to identify the person or persons responsible for ensuring that data are properly obtained and analyzed. As students' needs advance to interventions that are more intensive, school psychologists, special education teachers, educational staff associates (ESAs), or other specialists may be called upon to manage, interpret, and synthesize student data to support decision-making teams.

In an RTI approach, the role of the school psychologist may change from traditional assessor of individual cognitive abilities to a more intervention-based assessor of target skills. School psychologists, in addition to ESAs and special education teachers, will need to assist the classroom teacher in using screening data and progress monitoring data to guide curriculum decisions. They will need to assist the decision-making team in using assessment data to identify specific curriculum areas of concern. This means that school psychologists will need to be knowledgeable about available interventions. School psychologists will also be needed to incorporate RTI data and analyze all available data to appropriately guide the special education referral process and eligibility decision. They should be particularly active in the analysis and interpretation of data as well as the standardization of local measures.

Effective leadership is obviously required to implement RTI change processes within the school. This leadership can take many forms. Principals often play a critical leadership role, but so can teachers and other staff, including those in the district office. In order to be effective leaders, principals must understand and be active in the change process. To assist teachers and support staff in providing instruction and interventions, they must provide or coordinate valuable and sustained professional development. Principals should have a hands-on role in making decisions within a problem-solving process. They should ensure that RTI practices are implemented with fidelity and that student data are managed properly.

Question #24: What Does the RTI Process Mean for Teachers?

An RTI outcome vital to the effectiveness of a school system is that *all teachers*, both general and special educators, will feel an increased accountability for student learning as well as strengthened confidence in their own skills and knowledge related to teaching reading. The goal of all students learning to read will be a unifying force that includes all staff and all students. All teachers will see themselves as part of a system that delivers high-quality instruction that continually assesses student progress and provides extra help and extra time to meet students' needs.

If we are to close the achievement gap in schools, roles of school personnel will change. Collaboration among teachers will increase in order to determine students, needs, designate resources, and maximize student learning. Genuine access to and participation in the general curriculum for students with disabilities may require a shift in the way we think about and ultimately provide special education and related services. Building better readers must become the collective responsibility of all teachers so that all students achieve.

Although RTI presents a promising way of addressing many issues associated with SLD identification, unanswered implementation questions remain. We must ask how many issues relevant to SLD determination are due to the specific assessment components, as well as to the limited fidelity with which those components were implemented (e.g., appropriate learning experiences, prereferral intervention, application of exclusion clause, and aptitude-achievement discrepancy). Further, we must consider how well states, districts, and schools could implement an assessment process that incorporates significant changes in staff roles and responsibilities (i.e., most dramatically for general education staff), while lengthening the duration of disability determination assessment and possibly lengthening service time.

Another significant consideration is that current research literature provides scant scientific evidence on how RTI applies in curricular areas other than reading and beyond primary or elementary school-age children. In conjunction with the standards that have been developed (by the National Committee on Science Education Standards and Assessment [NCSESA], 1996, and the National Council of Teachers of Mathematics [NCTM], 2000), science-based research needs to be conducted using the RTI construct in the areas of science and mathematics. Utilizing an RTI framework across educational disciplines as well as grade levels is synergistic with the No Child Left Behind Act of 2001 and promotes the idea that schools have an obligation to ensure that all students participate in strong instructional programs that support multifaceted learning.

Although RTI represents a promising way of addressing many issues associated with SLD identification, unanswered implementation questions remain. We must ask how many issues relevant to SLD determination are due to the specific assessment components, as well as the limited fidelity with which those components have been implemented. Further, we must consider how well schools could implement an assessment process that incorporates significant changes in staff roles and responsibilities while lengthening the duration of disability determination assessment.

Question #25: What Do Teachers Need in Terms of Professional Development and RTI?

Teachers of students with learning disabilities will need to acquire specialized knowledge to individualize instruction, to build skills, and to recommend modifications and accommodations needed for students with learning disabilities to be successful in the general curriculum.

Within the RTI framework, professional development will be needed to prepare these teachers to be able to

- understand and apply pedagogy related to cognition, learning theory, language development, behavior management, and applied behavioral analysis;
- possess a substantial base of knowledge about criteria for identifying scientific, research-based methodology, instructional programs/methodology available for use with students with learning disabilities, and individualization of instruction;
- be proficient in providing direct skill instruction in reading, writing, spelling, math, and listening and learning strategies;
- be able to adjust instruction and learning supports based on student progress, observation, and clinical judgment;
- conduct comprehensive evaluations that include standardized assessment measures, informal assessment, and behavioral observations;
- translate the data into meaningful educational recommendations;
- explain test results to help parents and teachers understand the student's needs and the recommendations generated during the assessment process;
- possess strong communication skills to function as collaborative partners and members of problem solving teams; and
- be knowledgeable about the legal requirements of IDEA 2004, federal and state regulations, and the history of learning disabilities.

(Division for Learning Disabilities, 2006)

Step II

Understanding Why RTI Plays an Important Role in the Determination of Specific Learning Disabilities

Question #26: How Does IDEA 2004 Define a Specific Learning Disability?

IDEA 2004 continues to define *specific learning disability* (SLD) as "a disorder in one or more of the basic psychological processes involved in understanding or in using language, spoken, or written, which disorder may manifest itself in the imperfect ability to listen, think, speak, write, spell, or do mathematical calculations." The term includes "conditions such as perceptual disabilities, brain injury, minimal brain dysfunction, dyslexia, and developmental aphasia." The term does not include "a learning problem that is primarily the result of visual, hearing, or motor disabilities, of mental retardation, of emotional disturbance, or of environmental, cultural, or economic disadvantage."

Question #27: How Have Children Been Identified Under the Category of Specific Learning Disabilities?

The process for determining the presence of an SLD has involved the use of an intelligence-achievement discrepancy criterion for many years. This method has been widely criticized as the "wait-to-fail" method since students rarely qualify for special education services until third or fourth grade. Intensive reading instruction is often delayed until well after typically developing readers have mastered the reading process. Furthermore, the discrepancy model does not necessarily distinguish between those students who fail due to inadequate reading instruction and those who possess disorders in one or more of the psychological processes involved in using language and manifested in the imperfect ability to listen, think, speak, read, write, spell, or do mathematical calculations.

Question #28: What Events Led to Changes in LD Identification in IDEA 2004?

Through decades of educational practice, it has become generally accepted that a "severe discrepancy" is *in fact* a learning disability (LD) and/or a proxy for an LD and its underlying processing disorders. It is now widely acknowledged that there is not a scientific basis for the use of a measured IQ-achievement discrepancy as either a defining characteristic of or a marker for an LD. Though numerous authorities (Fletcher et al., 1998; Lyon et al., 2001; Stanovich, 2005) have identified problems with discrepancy models, it has persisted as the most widely used diagnostic concept. In the 1997 reauthorization process, the concern with discrepancy approaches reached a head and the U.S. Office of Special Education Programs (OSEP) committed to a vigorous program of examining and summarizing evidence around LD identification. That effort resulted in the Learning Disabilities Summit, as well as subsequent roundtable meetings involving representatives of major professional organizations. While preparing for the 2004 IDEA reauthorization, OSEP conducted the 2002 Learning Disabilities Roundtable to generate a series of consensus statements about the field of LDs. With respect to the use of discrepancy formulas, the members stated, "Roundtable participants agree that there is no evidence that ability-achievement discrepancy formulas can be applied in a consistent and educationally meaning-ful (i.e., reliable and valid) manner. They believe SLD eligibility should not be operationalized using ability-achievement discrepancy formulas."

Question #29: Why Replace the Discrepancy Model With RTI?

RTI offers the promise of "building better readers" through the pro-vision of differentiated instruction based on data from ongoing assessments for all students in the early grades. That is, all students receive scientific, research-based reading instruction, and most important, struggling readers receive additional instructional time and research-based reading interventions within the structure and context of the general education classroom. In essence, RTI replaces the practice of waiting to fail with deliberate early intervention and prevention.

Question #30: What Are Major Issues Related to the Use of the Concept of Ability-Achievement Discrepancy? Why Change?

Issue #1

Discrepancy models fail to differentiate between children who have LDs and those who have academic achievement problems related to poor instruction, lack of experience, or other problems.

It is generally agreed that the model of ability-achievement dis-crepancy that has been employed was influenced by research con-ducted by Rutter and Yule (1975, as cited in Reschly, 2003). This research found two groups of low-achieving readers, one with dis-crepancies and one without. This finding formed the basis for the idea that a discrepancy was meaningful for both classification and treatment purposes. Later analyses of this research, and attempts to replicate it, have failed to produce support for the "two group" model for either purpose. In fact, it is now accepted that reading occurs in a normal distribution and that students with dyslexia or severe reading problems represent the lower end of that distribution (Fletcher et al., 2002).

Issue #2

Discrepancy models discriminate against certain groups of students: students outside of "mainstream" culture and students who are in the upper and lower ranges of IQ.

Due to psychometric problems, discrepancy approaches tend to underidentify children at the lower end of the IQ range and over-identify children at the upper end. This problem has been addressed by various formulas that correct for the regression to the mean that occurs when two correlated measures are used. However, using regression formulas does not address issues such as language and cultural bias in IQ tests, nor does it improve the classification function of a discrepancy model (Stuebing et al., 2002).

Issue #3

Discrepancy models do not effectively predict which students will benefit from or respond differentially to instruction.

The research around this issue has examined both progress and absolute outcomes for children with and without discrepancy, and has not supported the notion the two groups will respond differentially to instruction (Stanovich, 2005). Poor readers with discrepancies and poor readers without discrepancies perform similarly on skills considered important to the development of reading skills (Gresham, 2002).

Issue #4

The use of discrepancy models requires children to fail for a substantial period—usually years—before they are far enough behind to exhibit a discrepancy.

In order for children to exhibit a discrepancy, two tests need to be administered—an IQ test such as the Wechsler Intelligence Scale for Children and an achievement test such as a Woodcock-Johnson Tests of Achievement. Because of limitations of achievement and IQ testing, discrepancies often do not "appear" until late second, third, or even fourth grade. Educators and parents have experienced the frustration of knowing a child's skills are not adequate and not typical of the child's overall functioning and of being told to "wait a year" to rerefer the child. While waiting for a discrepancy to appear, other persistent problems associated with school failure develop such as poor self-concept, compromised motivation, vocabulary deficits, and deficits associated with limited access to written content.

Question #31: Why Was RTI Considered in the Process of SLD Determination?

RTI is being strongly considered as part of the SLD identification process because it has the potential to address areas of the SLD definition and construct that are not adequately assessed with current approaches. If the features of RTI are implemented correctly,

- there is some assurance that students are being exposed to high-quality instruction in the general education classroom by stipulating that schools use evidence-based instructional practices and routinely monitor the progress of all students;
- there is an emphasis on underachievement through its focus on discrepancy models that examine whether a student is failing to respond to instruction through both low overall achievement and inability to make adequate progress;
- they encourage access to early intervention because, with the regular monitoring of progress, at-risk students are identified early, and an infrastructure for the appropriate delivery of services already is established;
- they are designed to address many students with achievement problems, so the label of "LD" is applied only for those students who fail to respond to multiple levels of intervention efforts; and
- they are meant to be applied as multiple measures of child performance rather than as limiting determination to a single point in time.

Question #32: Today, What Role Should RTI Play in the Identification of Children With a Specific Learning Disability?

When considering adopting an RTI approach for identifying students with SLDs, school districts should keep in mind a number of provisions of IDEA 2004. Under IDEA 2004, schools districts may, but are no longer required to, consider whether a student has a severe discrepancy between achievement and intellectual ability. At the same time, IDEA 2004 gives school districts the flexibility to determine that a student has an SLD using RTI data. Proponents point out that identifying SLDs through RTI shifts the focus of the evaluation process from emphasizing the documentation of the student's disability to emphasizing the student's instructional needs. RTI emphasizes this shift of focus through documentation of a student's persistent failure to progress even after receiving intense and sound scientific-research-based interventions in the general education curriculum.

IDEA 2004 is silent about the exact criteria school districts may use in establishing an SLD. It is expected that when final federal regulations are published, specific criteria will be established and states will be provided clarifying guidance regarding these procedures. Until that time, districts implementing RTI are strongly encouraged to use established approaches for using RTI data to identify SLDs. The following is recommended.

After appropriate curriculum-based measurement (CBM) probes have been applied and after attempts have been made to implement at least two Tier 3 interventions with fidelity, a student should be considered nonresponsive when (a) the student's level of academic achievement has been determined to be significantly lower than that of his or her peers and (b) the gap between the student's achievement and that of his or her peers increases (or does not significantly decrease). Absent other information to explain the lack of achievement, students who are nonresponsive at Tier 3 should be suspected of having a disability.

Once a referral for 504 or special education is initiated, the school district must determine whether an initial comprehensive evaluation is required to determine the presence of a disability. Unless mitigating information exists to explain why the student was nonresponsive at Tier 3, it is anticipated that an initial evaluation will be completed. Before conducting an initial evaluation, the school district must obtain written consent from a parent or guardian. A comprehensive evaluation may or may not require additional testing. A comprehensive evaluation should include a formal observation of the student by a team member unless a recent observation was completed by a team member prior to the evaluation. If the student's evaluation team is able to determine that the existing data developed through the RTI process is sufficient to complete the evaluation report in all suspected areas of disability, additional information does not need to be obtained. If the existing data does not establish the need for special education services, further assessment may be needed to rule out the possibility of a qualifying disability including a disability in a category other than SLDs.

Question #33: Can RTI Be Used as the Sole Determinant for SLD Classification?

While RTI addresses some significant shortcomings in current approaches to SLD identification and other concerns about early identification of students at risk for reading problems, RTI should be considered as merely one important element within the larger context of the SLD determination process. Implementing RTI allows schools to have more confidence that they are providing appropriate learning experiences to all students while identifying and targeting early those students who may be at risk for reading or math problems but who do not necessarily have an LD. Although IDEA 2004 provides flexibility to LEAs in determining SLD identification procedures, the following recommendations by the National Joint Committee on Learning Disabilities (NJCLD, 2005) should help guide the development of these procedures:

> Decisions regarding eligibility for special education services must draw from information collected from a comprehensive individual evaluation using multiple methods including clinical judgment and other sources of relevant information. Students must be evaluated on an individual basis and assessed for intraindividual differences in the seven domains that comprise the definition of SLD in the law—listening, thinking, speaking, reading, writing, spelling, and mathematical calculation. Eligibility decisions must be made through an interdisciplinary team, must be student-centered and informed by appropriate data, and must be based on student needs and strengths.

As schools begin to execute a process of decision making that is more clinical than statistical in nature, ensuring through regulations that this team of qualified professionals represents all competencies necessary for accurate review of comprehensive assessment data will be critical.

One of the advantages of RTI is the timely identification of children who struggle with learning. While RTI is not intended as a stand-alone approach to determining SLDs, it can be a key component of a comprehensive approach to disability determination. In an RTI model, if a student does not respond to robust high-quality instruction and intervention that is progress monitored over time, he or she may indeed be determined to have an LD. The benefit of RTI for these at-risk students is that it provides a wealth of meaningful instructional data that can be used in creating well-targeted individualized instructional programs and evidence-based instructional interventions. In addition, RTI sets in place a student progress monitoring process that facilitates communication and promotes ongoing meaningful dialogue between home and school.

Question #34: Are There Other Indicators of LDs That Are More Valid and Reliable?

Generally, attempts to reliably define and measure psychological processing difficulties have yielded limited results that render them without practical application. However, related to this research, certain skills have been identified as robust predictors of academic performance. These skills may be characterized as "critical indicators" or "marker variables." When embracing this approach, one accepts that the indicator may represent both constitutional *and* learned skills and that the variable represents an important capability. Using this approach, researchers have identified measures of phonological awareness and early literacy knowledge such as letter sound relationships as powerful early predictors of later reading performance (Good & Kaminski, 2002). Similarly, fluent reading of connected text continues to be highly correlated with growth in both word reading and comprehension, and represents meaningful ways to screen and progress monitor in reading (L. S. Fuchs & D. Fuchs, 1998). Using this approach provides a method of screening to identify students with potentially persistent academic problems and assessing them further.

Fortunately, these variables have been identified for the most prevalent of school-identified LD, those in the area of reading. Similar measures for domains such as math reasoning, calculation, and written language have not been as thoroughly investigated.

Use of these indicators is a key practice that underlies the RTI approach. Since they are valid measures of current performance and good predictors of later performance, they can be used to prevent the most serious of problems with discrepancy models—the problem of waiting for children to fail before they receive help.

Question #35: If Authorities Believe Underlying Processing Disorders Are the Cause of Learning Disabilities, Why Doesn't IDEA 2004 Include a Model Based on Measuring Processing Problems?

It is a relatively common practice for LD assessment to include descriptions of "processing" or "patterns of cognitive ability." Frequently, the conclusions that are made are based on a student's performance on subtests of intelligence measures, memory tests, and language evaluations. While interesting results may sometimes be produced, drawing conclusions about the presence of a disability based on such results is not substantiated by research (Fletcher et al., 1998; Torgeson, 2002).

Assessment of processing deficits in order to diagnose LDs has a history even longer than that of discrepancy approaches. Indeed, frustration with the reliability and validity of processing assessment contributed to the proposal to use the severe discrepancy in LD criteria (Hallahan & Mercer, 2002). The result was the inclusion of the concept of processing deficits in the federal definition of LD, but no criteria related to processing. There are clear advantages to this approach that make continued focus on processing variables attractive for both research and practice. Of particular importance is the concept that, if direct assessment of intrinsic processing was possible, so might be early and intensive preventative education that would avoid the associated pitfalls of school failure.

In other words, it is not possible to separate out all of the complicated factors that contribute to a child's performance on tasks and make the assumption that an intrinsic cognitive process is being measured. While there may be promising research under way, a methodology for discrete diagnosis or classification based on processing differences is unavailable and certainly could not be included in LD criteria. At this time, it is probably appropriate to follow the advice of McGrady (2002) and continue a research program for assessment of intrinsic processes independent of school practice.

Processes for SLD identification have changed and will continue to do so over time. Within that context, remembering that RTI is but one resource for use in the SLD determination process is important. More broadly speaking, RTI procedures have the distinction that when implemented with fidelity, they can identify and intervene for students early in the educational process, thereby reducing academic failure among all students.

Question #36: In the Big Picture, How Does RTI Fit Into the Determination of LD Process?

Although RTI addresses some significant shortcomings in current approaches to SLD identification and other concerns about early identification of students at risk for reading problems, RTI should be considered one important element within the larger context of the SLD determination process. RTI as one component of SLD determination is insufficient as a sole criterion for accurately determining SLD. RTI provides the following information about a student:

1. Indication of the student's skill level relative to peers or a criterion benchmark

2. Success or lack of success of particular interventions

3. Sense of the intensity of instructional supports that will be necessary for the student to achieve

Incorporating this information into SLD determination procedures has the potential to make important contributions to identifying students with SLD in schools. In addition to an RTI process that helps ensure appropriate learning experiences and early intervention, identification of SLD should include a student-centered, comprehensive evaluation that ensures students who have an LD are accurately identified.

Although IDEA 2004 provides flexibility to LEAs in determining SLD identification procedures, the following recommendations by the NJCLD (2005) should help guide the development of these procedures:

- Decisions regarding eligibility for special education services must draw from information collected from a comprehensive individual evaluation using multiple methods including clinical judgment and other sources of relevant information.
- Students must be evaluated on an individual basis and assessed for intraindividual differences in the seven domains that comprise the definition of SLD in the law: listening,

thinking, speaking, reading, writing, spelling, and mathematical calculation.

- Eligibility decisions must be made through an interdisciplinary team, must be student centered and informed by appropriate data, and must be based on student needs and strengths.
- As schools begin to execute a process of decision making that is more clinical than statistical in nature, ensuring through regulations that this team of qualified professionals represents all competencies necessary for accurate review of comprehensive assessment data will be critical.

Processes for SLD identification have changed and will continue to do so. Within that context, remembering that RTI is but one resource for use in the SLD determination process is important. More broadly speaking, RTI procedures have the distinction that when implemented with fidelity, they can identify and intervene for students early in the educational process, thereby reducing academic failure among students.

Step III

Determining Your School's Capacity to Adopt RTI

Question #37: What Basic Decisions Should a School or District Make Before Implementing RTI?

Of primary importance is an assurance that school staff and school and district leaders are committed to making RTI work to address the needs of struggling readers. Educators must recognize the need for a different and more powerful way of teaching reading to guarantee that all students learn how to read.

After the initial commitment is made, a school or school district must focus on implementing initial and sustained professional development for teachers on the five critical components of early reading. Other issues, no less important, that must be discussed and resolved include how to optimize the use of staff time and student time, how to provide the materials necessary for scientifically based core instruction and targeted intervention, how to ensure funding, and how to provide ongoing leadership and support as RTI is established in the school and district.

Before implementation of one of the many RTI models can begin in a district, several basic decisions must be made about the structure and components to be selected, as well as how students will move through the process.

Selecting Structure and Components

The most basic decision is selecting and defining the specific structure and components of the service-delivery system that will be used. Current RTI implementation models use a generally similar structure with some common components, but they also show variations. Some initiatives include relatively rigid tiers, while in others the number of tiers varies in different school districts, depending on resources and other factors. For example, a district might adopt a "standard protocol" model with two fairly rigid tiers (e.g., a single type of remedial program as the sole basis for assessing RTI) or a multitiered model having three, more flexible tiers. The model and components selected will influence the personnel, resources, and decision-making processes to be implemented.

Balancing Rigidity and Flexibility

As RTI models become more widely implemented in schools, questions are being raised about the degree of rigidity or flexibility built into the implementation. A relatively stable framework involving greater consistency across schools, districts, and states may increase the opportunity and likelihood that successful models can be researched and replicated. Flexibility in timelines and structure, however, can be more responsive to the uniquely individual needs of students with learning disabilities (LDs) and can maximize problem-solving opportunities.

That flexibility requires staff with a broad range of skills and competencies who are comfortable in a less structured environment. The flexible approach also makes both meaningful research and replication more problematic. The flexibility-rigidity decision can be expected to affect the degree of student individualization, the sophistication required of personnel, the cost of staff resources, the suitability for meaningful research, and the likelihood of replication.

Movement Within and Between Tiers

At present, there is little agreement or data about what specific criteria or cut scores optimize decisions about movement through the tiers. Similarly, the mandate that scientific, researched-based instruction be used limits the choices for beginning reading instruction and raises difficult questions about instructional options in such areas as mathematics, reading comprehension, and written expression, in which few scientific, research-based interventions exist at the elementary or secondary level.

Intervention Fidelity and Other Instructional Issues

Major challenges to implementation of an RTI model are decisions about selecting and monitoring research-based interventions that are matched to students and implemented with fidelity and appropriate intensity, frequency, and duration. Other instructional issues that must be resolved include the environments in which various interventions will be provided and the people who will provide the interventions. In addition, the scheduling and the time required for the team decision-making processes, programs, interventions, and supports need to be resolved.

Question #38: What Approaches Are Available for Implementing RTI?

Several organizational approaches are available for implementing RTI. These models generally encompass the following four system requirements (Gresham, 2002; Vaughn, 2002):

1. Measurement of academic growth

2. Use of validated interventions

3. Capability of distinguishing between (a) performance deficits and skill deficits and (b) instructional problems and individual learning problems

4. Ability to determine the effects of interventions and make decisions about cutoff criteria

These requirements imply both technical and practical capacity that must be considered when an RTI system is developed or adopted.

Question #39: How Do You Measure Academic Growth?

Fuchs and Fuchs (1998) introduced the important concept that a student, in order to be considered to have a learning disability, must be *dually discrepant.* It has been demonstrated that, in order for a student to be reliably classified as having an

LD, low achievement must be accompanied by slow progress. Using low achievement alone results in group membership that will change substantially over time, with students moving into and out of the group (Francis et al., 2005).

RTI decisions must be made both on the basis of a student's relative low achievement and on the student's slow slope of progress. These criteria can be met by use of a well-documented approach referred to as *curriculum-based measurement* (CBM; Fuchs & Fuchs, 1998). Curriculum-based measurement uses "critical indicators" of growth such as oral reading fluency, correct word sequences written, and rate of correct calculations. These measures may be normalized on a local sample (Shinn, 1988) or on the results of large-scale studies. Alternatively, typical peers may be sampled as a direct comparison group during the assessment phase (Fuchs & Fuchs, 1998). CBMs have been established as valid, easy to use, and economical. They can also be used as frequently as daily without threatening their sensitivity.

One should note that RTI research and model implementation generally focus on elementary-aged children. The measures that are available are most appropriately used with younger students and, as students mature, factors such as motivation and behavior make interpretation of students' performance increasingly complex. This is true of traditional testing paradigms as well. RTI models frequently combine response to intervention with hypothesis-testing or problem-solving approaches, both of which become increasingly important for older students. For students in late elementary and secondary schools, careful review of students' histories is very important.

Question #40: How Do You Use Validated Interventions?

General education is the first intervention. Many authors (e.g., Kame'enui & Simmons, 2002) conceptualize the first phase of "intervention" to be at the general education basic or core curriculum level. From this perspective, use of a research-based core curriculum is a necessary precondition for adopting RTI.

Such curricula provide development in the instructional components identified as essential by the National Reading Panel: phonemic awareness, systematic phonics, fluency, vocabulary, and text comprehension. A number of published curricula have been aligned with these instructional components. An issue for consideration in an RTI model is that there should be a mechanism in place for judging the fidelity of implementation of any identified curriculum.

Research supports interventions. With respect to more intensive individual interventions, the body of literature on validated procedures is growing. Gresham (2002) reviewed the current body of literature and reached the following conclusions:

1. Research supports the concept of a validated intervention protocol.

2. A combination of "direct instruction" and "strategy instruction" is the most productive in effecting growth.

The use of validated instructional protocols presumes that the school has identified sets of instructional interventions, usually of increasing intensity, that have been demonstrated to be effective. These interventions vary by curriculum focus, group size, frequency, duration, and motivational conditions.

Often these variables are modified in relation to student characteristics. Using direct instruction and strategy instruction means the school has adopted interventions based on these well-established instructional approaches.

Direct instruction models are characterized by relatively more teacher-directed instruction and less independent seatwork. Information is carefully structured and sequenced and is actively presented so as to maximize student attention, involvement, and practice. Consistent procedures for cueing, prompting, and correction are utilized within the context of ongoing assessment of student understanding (Huitt, 1996). In direct instruction models, student mastery is carefully defined and achieved before moving to the next step in the instructional sequence.

Strategy instruction employs specific, highly elaborated instruction in text comprehension. Validated models of strategy instruction use instructional techniques that are consistent with direct instruction. Modeling and planned generalization of skills are typical instructional steps in strategy instruction. Several authors (e.g., Pressley, 2000) have described instructional sequences appropriate to strategy instruction.

Question #41: How Do You Distinguish Between Types of Learning and Performance Problems?

Gresham (2002) described relevant research demonstrating that it is possible to determine if a student's problems are performance problems (can do, but does not) or instructional problems (was not taught or was not available for teaching). In the case of performance problems, an intervention might alter the motivational conditions (contingencies associated with) of a task. Howell and Nolet (2000) detailed a number of ways to alter instructional conditions to assess the effects of motivation and other variables on acquisition of knowledge. In the case of instructional problems, the larger instructional context might be analyzed more thoroughly—for example, assessing the growth trends of all children in a class or grade level—to determine if there is a curriculum and instruction problem contributing to skill acquisition for the group as a whole.

These distinctions are often made within the context of what is termed a *problem-solving approach*. In this approach, hypotheses are developed that "compete" with the explanation that a child has a disability. These hypotheses are tested first by providing interventions that address the problem identified and then by evaluating the student's progress. For example, frequently changing schools is often a contributor to students' struggles. In a problem-solving approach, the student might be provided with a moderately intense reading program at an appropriate curricular level. By carefully tracking the student's progress, the team might conclude that the student's strong response is an indicator that interrupted instruction—rather than the existence of a learning disability—is a reasonable explanation for the student's academic struggles.

Question #42: How Do You Determine the Effects of Instruction and Make Decisions About Cutoff Criteria?

When beginning to use RTI, the first question practitioners often ask is, "How much progress is enough?" The second question, closely following, is, "When is an intervention *special* education?"

Success in answering the first question is predicated on the ability to sensitively measure growth and to know what benchmark the student is working toward. Research in applied behavior analysis and curriculum-based measurement informs the practices necessary to track the effects of interventions. A regular, reliable progress monitoring tool such as an oral reading fluency measure must be adopted. The school must also know what is expected of the typically progressing student. Data must be plotted and reviewed, and decisions must be made when the data are examined. Most systems develop decision-making rules to guide this process. For example, a decision-making rule might be, "Change the intervention after one week of data points that do not meet the student's aim line."

The second question, "When is an intervention *special* education?" is one that involves a system-level decision as well as a clinical decision. First, a socially determined cutoff for "functional" performance must be established. This is usually defined as the "average" range on a normal distribution. Second, an informed group of professionals needs to evaluate the intensity of the intervention provided and either test or make a professional judgment about the effect of removing an intensive intervention.

Question #43: What Are the Different Types of Response to Intervention Models?

A number of models have been utilized to implement RTI. Various authors have labeled their approaches as being of a specific type—such as those described in the following discussion—but, in reality, the approaches share similarities. For example, the problem-solving model is used at certain points in the tiered model. Both the problem-solving and tiered models may involve direct teacher referral to teams that may result in a form of what has been thought of as pre-referral intervention.

Question #44: What Is Problem Solving or Hypothesis Testing?

Problem-solving approaches typically involve a team of teachers who engage in a systematic process of problem identification and intervention implementation.

The underlying assumption in problem solving is that the presence of a disability is the least likely and therefore least common explanation for failure.

In problem-solving approaches, teams of teachers and other specialists will typically review a student's history and known attributes in an attempt to identify issues other than disability that would explain the student's failure. Problems a teacher or team investigates could include interrupted school experiences caused by frequent moving or illness, lack of student "availability" for instruction due to trauma or behavioral challenges, inadequate previous instruction, or the presence of other disabilities.

Marston, Canter, Lau, and Muyskens (2002) described the widespread use of the problem-solving approach in the Minneapolis public school system. This system uses problem solving within the context of "Intervention Assistance Teams." In Minneapolis, general education teachers are trained to identify problems, design interventions, and determine whether their interventions are effective. If they are not, the Intervention Assessment Team assists in developing and providing other interventions. If those interventions fail, the student is referred to a "Student Support Team" for a special education evaluation. This system relies heavily on the capacity of its general and special education teachers to use CBMs to track student progress and has well defined procedures for moving students through levels of intervention.

In order for a problem-solving approach to meet the general Individuals with Disabilities Education Improvement Act (IDEA) of 2004 evaluation requirements, meet RTI requirements, and overcome shortcomings associated with more traditional assessment models, schools must adopt the following system components:

1. Use of decision rules to prompt referral

2. Adopted standards for intervention design

3. Uniform progress monitoring procedures

4. Decision rules for judging effectiveness of interventions

The following is a summary of the relative strengths and challenges inherent in a "pure" problem-solving approach:

Strengths

- Problem-solving approaches address the "exclusionary" requirements of LD evaluation.
- A problem-solving approach fits easily into systems that many schools already have in place, such as teacher assistance teams.

- Problem-solving approaches may not require the adoption of extensive new assessment technology.
- Educationally relevant information may be gathered throughout the process.

Challenges

- Identified problems are often ones that schools cannot directly address.
- Academic problems induced by external factors such as lack of preschool experience or behavior difficulties may coexist with learning disabilities.
- Problem-solving models alone do not address problems like referral bias.

Question #45: What Are Prereferral Approaches?

Prereferral models were conceived in the 1980s as a method of addressing overidentification in special education through prevention of inappropriate referrals. Essentially, this model systematizes requirements that general education teachers modify instructional and classroom management approaches in order to better meet the needs of diverse learners. Through prereferral, teachers are guided to differentiate instruction in order to maximize the number of students who benefit from the general education program.

The most typical prereferral models have at their heart a teacher assistance team, known by a variety of names including care teams, student study teams, and student assistance teams. The team processes cases of students who are identified by their teachers as struggling. The team may design specific interventions or make suggestions to the teacher for possible interventions. If positive results are documented, no referral is made to special education. If, however, a lack of improvement is noted, the student is referred for a special education evaluation.

Major shortcomings of the prereferral model for use in RTI include referral bias and negative perceptions of the process among classroom teachers. Factors such as teachers' years of training and experience and the socioeconomic status of students have been shown to influence which students are identified as struggling (Drame, 2002). Referrals may be based as much on how overwhelmed teachers are feeling at any given moment as on a student's level of skill development or performance. Additionally, the prereferral process can be viewed as a series of hoops through which a teacher must jump before being "allowed" to make a special education referral rather than a meaningful avenue for addressing students' needs (Slonski-Fowler & Truscott, 2004).

Perhaps the most significant drawback of a prereferral model is that the teacher must deal with each struggling student individually. Given that up to 20 percent of students are likely to have significant difficulty learning to read (Shaywitz, 2004), this approach makes it difficult to provide meaningful resources to all students.

While it is likely that students with the most apparent and immediate needs will be referred for interventions, intervening with students one by one forces teachers into educational triage. Meanwhile, students with marginal problems will continue to struggle and perhaps fall further behind (Gerber & Semmel, 1984; Gresham, MacMillan, & Bocian, 1997).

Prereferral models may be more or less prescriptive with respect to decision rules for identifying students, intervention design, and progress monitoring. Many of the model's weaknesses can be addressed by adopting standard practices that are designed and monitored by the teacher assistance team.

Adopting procedures to ensure uniformity in decision making is critical to utilization of a prereferral model for RTI. Without specific system components, a prereferral system will not meet the general IDEA 2004 evaluation requirements or the RTI requirements and will fail to remedy the shortcomings of traditional assessment paradigms.

Prereferral strengths and challenges include the following:

Strengths

- Many school districts currently have prereferral systems in place.
- Prereferral utilizes a team approach to identifying students.
- Prereferral provides for systematic response to students' difficulties before evaluation.
- Prereferral has the potential to build capacity for individual teachers to differentiate instruction for struggling learners.
- It may be combined with typical components of other models, such as problem solving approaches.
- Educationally relevant information is gathered throughout the process.

Challenges

- Prereferral does not inherently address the problem of referral bias, as it depends on idiosyncratic responses of teachers to academic difficulty.
- Traditionally, prereferral models do not use a prescribed intervention protocol.
- The reporting of effects of intervention is often anecdotal and lacks standard format for data presentation.
- Students are dealt with "one at a time," which may delay intervention to students with less severe deficits.

Question #46: What Is Tiered Intervention?

The three-tiered model is based on literature in the area of public health (Caplan & Grunebaum, 1967) and positive behavior support (Walker et al., 1996). Using the public health analogy, systematic practices for healthy individuals (strong and normally developing readers) and those at risk of developing health conditions (students showing early signs of struggling) will prevent severe problems from developing and will also allow for identification of individuals with the potential to develop severe problems.

The underlying assumption of this prevention-oriented approach is that approximately 80 percent of students will benefit from implementation of a research-based core curriculum program that is being delivered with a high degree of fidelity. This level of intervention is referred to as "primary" or "Tier 1." An estimated 15 percent of students will need additional intervention support beyond the core curriculum ("secondary" or "Tier 2") , and about 5 percent who have not responded to primary and secondary efforts may require more intensive, individualized support ("tertiary" or "Tier 3" level).

This approach requires the use of a universal screening program. The three-tiered model has been implemented successfully in Oregon as the *Effective Behavior and Instructional Support* system (Sadler, 2002). In this model, teams of teachers examine a standard set of data that is gathered on a periodic schedule. Students are sorted into groups that are provided with increasingly intensive interventions depending on their achievement and response to intervention. Movement through the tiers is a dynamic process, with students entering and exiting according to their progress data.

In this model, it is assumed that students who do not respond to the most intensive intervention are likely to have a learning disability. Frequently, the tiered approach is combined with more traditional assessment models or with problem-solving procedures before a student is determined to have a disability.

This approach requires "blurring" of the lines between general and special education, as well as close cooperation or merging of compensatory education services and services for English language learners.

Relative strengths and challenges of the tiered model include the following:

Strengths

- All struggling students are identified. Prevention and early identification are possible.
- Students may be "sorted" into levels of severity, and interventions may be tailored to each group.
- Decision making is based on standardized progress monitoring information.
- Intervention decisions can be standardized.
- It may be combined with typical components of other models, such as problem-solving approaches.
- Educationally relevant information is gathered throughout the process.

Challenges

- Resources must be committed for universal screening.
- It requires skill grouping across classes to provide interventions of sufficient intensity.
- Ensuring that every child at risk is identified and provided intervention requires establishment of broad groupings, which may result in allocation of resources on children who are not actually in need.
- The most suitable screening and progress monitoring tools are available in reading. Tools in other areas are not as well established.

Question #47: What Resources Are Necessary to Implement an RTI Approach?

To implement an RTI approach, many questions about ensuring adequate resources must first be resolved. Some of the challenges that must be addressed are as follows.

Time

Implementation of an RTI approach can be expected to create a need for decisions about adjustments in daily student, teacher, and administrative schedules and time for decision-making team meetings to be incorporated into school, personnel, and parent schedules. Time for professional development will need to be allotted both prior to adopting a new approach and on an ongoing basis. Other critical decisions concern timelines for the phasing in of an RTI approach, the establishment of timelines for the minimum and maximum time a student may spend in various tiers, and how much time will be given to specific instruction or intervention efforts.

Space and Materials

An important part of successful implementation of an RTI approach is provision of needed space and materials. These will include space for conducting intensive small group or tutoring interventions as well as the materials and technology required for professional development, evidence-based and intensive instruction, progress monitoring, evaluation, and record keeping.

Documentation

For school personnel there will be increased paperwork due to data collection and documentation demands for the progress monitoring, classification criteria, movement between levels, intervention documentation, and other record keeping that are critical for following the progress of individual students in an RTI approach. The President's Commission on Excellence in Special Education (2002) identified the amount of paperwork as the main cause of dissatisfaction among special education teachers. How much this would be ameliorated by the availability and use of computers and other technological devices and assistance from paraprofessionals, however, remains an unresolved question.

Financial Support

Although several RTI models have been implemented in various parts of the United States, there is very little information available about the comparative costs of RTI with more traditional service-delivery models. The changing personnel needs, increased resource requirements, and added professional development activities typical of initial implementation of an RTI model, however, all suggest there will be increased costs, at least in the short term. Designated instructional services such as speech and language, occupational therapy, educational therapy, and psychological services will also need continued funding.

It has been proposed that special education funds be used by general education to cover the cost of intensified instruction for students who are falling behind. If the number of students in special education were not to decrease, resources for students who are in need of special education and related services would have to be curtailed unless additional funds are allocated.

Step IV

Screening for "At-Risk" Students

Question #48: What Is Screening?

Screening is a type of assessment that is characterized by providing quick, low-cost, repeatable testing of age-appropriate critical skills (e.g., identifying letters of the alphabet or reading a list of high-frequency words) or behaviors (e.g., tardiness, aggression, or hyper-activity).

The basic question in a screening measure is whether the student should be judged as "at risk." For example, the school nurse who uses the Snellen eye chart wants a quick indicator of students who might have difficulty seeing from a distance. If a student has difficulty reading the eye chart, a referral is made for a more in-depth assessment. In a similar way, the classroom teacher uses a screening measure to identify students who meet the screening criteria for possible at-risk status. These students are then considered for a more in-depth assessment such as monitoring their progress during the next six weeks with specific assessments.

For a screening measure to be useful, it should satisfy three criteria (Jenkins, 2003):

1. It needs to identify students who require further assessment.

2. It needs to be practical.

3. It needs to generate positive outcomes (accurately identifies students without consuming resources that could be put to better use).

Question #49: What Considerations Are Part of the Selection of Appropriate Screening Measures?

Accuracy

The main purpose of a screening instrument is to identify students whose performance on the measure warrants further investigation. Because screening does not directly result in diagnosis, it is better for a screening instrument to err on the side of false positives (students identified as at risk who, through more intense assessment, are found to have been misidentified) than on the side of false negatives (students not identified through screening who later turn out to be at risk). Therefore, a wider net with which to capture potentially at-risk students can be cast with screening measures. A potential drawback of having more false positives is the added expense of the additional testing and the provisions of services to more students, while a drawback of having more false negatives is that those students miss the opportunity to benefit from early intervention services. Ultimately, however, a school will want to find a measure that reaches an acceptable balance of efficiency and accuracy. To do this, schools will need to maintain data on how well the measure identifies students as at risk (e.g., track the number of false positives and false negatives). Such fine-tuning can help save resources.

One way to attempt to establish an acceptable balance is to use a decision-making model, which displays the distribution of true positives and true negatives, as well as the false positives and false negatives. A decision-making model also provides a mechanism for calculating the sensitivity and specificity of your screening tool. Sensitivity is the probability that the screening tool identifies those students who do have a specific learning disability (SLD), and specificity is the probability that the tool does not incorrectly identify those students who do not have an SLD.

Cut Score

Accuracy of screening also is determined by what cut scores are used. A cut score, also called a cut point, is the score that represents the dividing line between students who are not at risk and those who are potentially at risk. The goal of schoolwide screening is to identify those students who may be at risk for not acquiring the relevant skill and who may require further intervention. Schools will need to consider the emphasis given to particular levels of criteria performance when establishing cut scores. Additionally, some students perform on the "edge" of either side of the cut score, and guidelines will need to be established for determining when a student's performance warrants further investigation.

Criterion-Versus Norm-Referenced Measures

Screening measures can use either a criterion-referenced or normative comparison standard of performance. In the former, a specific criterion level of skills is specified as indicating an acceptable level of proficiency or mastery. In the normative comparison, the screening results are compared to an appropriate peer group (e.g., other students in first grade). Criterion measures are preferred because they give more accurate information about performance on relevant skills. In selecting an appropriate criterion measure, the school should attempt to link the measures at each grade level to appropriate existing performance measures including existing performance standards in the school's curriculum. The content will need to be relevant to age/grade level and the skill in question.

Efficiency

A screening procedure must be brief as well as simple enough to be implemented reliably by teachers. Teachers must view the procedures as reasonable and important, or they may not reliably implement them (Jenkins, 2003). Schoolwide training on implementation and schoolwide scheduling of screening procedures may be helpful in ensuring they are completed reliably.

Question #50: How Is Schoolwide Screening Done Within an RTI Model?

In the RTI model, screening is used to designate students who might be in need of closer monitoring in their general education curriculum or of a more intense intervention.

Screening is important as it represents the first gate or point of entry into subsequent tiers of RTI instruction. Screening is not a one-time process but an iterative system during the school year and across grade levels. During the course of primary instruction (Tier 1), the school uses schoolwide screening (consistency) in essential academic areas to identify each student's level of proficiency (usually three times per year). The screening data are organized to allow for comparison of both group and individual performance on specific skills (National Association of State Directors of Special Education [NASDSE], 2005).

In this way, the screening can serve three purposes:

1. Identify individuals in need of further assessment and possible movement to Tier 2 intervention

2. Provide feedback about class performance to help school leadership identify when a teacher might require support

3. If implemented on a regular basis across grade levels, identify false negatives—students who slip through the screening at one level but are then identified at later points in their school years.

The following excerpt from L. S. Fuchs and D. Fuchs (2006) summarizes the recommendations for best practice of schoolwide screening within an RTI model:

How to target students for preventative intervention [italics added]. Regardless of the number of tiers employed within the RTI system, a second procedural dimension concerns how students are targeted to enter the RTI process and receive preventative intervention. Some RTI systems employ one-time schoolwide screening, whereby all children in a school are assessed on a brief measure at the beginning of the school year. Students who score below a norm-referenced cut point (e.g., less than 25th percentile on the Woodcock Reading Mastery Tests—Word Identification) or below a performance benchmark associated with poor long-term outcome (e.g., less than 15 on curriculum-based measurement word identification fluency at the beginning of first grade) enter preventative intervention. In systems that rely on one-time schoolwide screening to identify students who enter preventative intervention, the assumption is that low performance relative to the normative cut point or the performance benchmark at the beginning of a school year constitutes evidence that the child has failed to respond to Tier 1 general education during previous school years and therefore requires preventative intervention.

In other versions of RTI, schoolwide screening is conducted to identify a subset of students whose response to Tier 1 general education is then monitored for a relatively short period of time to (dis)confirm the risk status indicated via schoolwide screening. Only the subset of students who (a) first meet the schoolwide screening cut point and (b) then evidence poor rates of improvement over five to eight weeks of Tier 1 general education are deemed in need of a preventative intervention.

Our recommendation is that schools use schoolwide screening in combination with at least five weeks of weekly progress monitoring in response to general education to identify students who require preventative intervention. Our rationale is that one-time universal screening at the beginning of the year can overidentify students who require preventative intervention. For example, in our research (Compton, Fuchs, Fuchs, & Bryant, 2006), conducted in reading at first grade, 50 percent of students identified on the basis of one-time screening spontaneously "recovered," i.e., made good progress over the course of first grade without preventative intervention. Identifying students for preventative intervention based on one-time screening means that schools are pressed to deliver costly preventative intervention to large numbers of students who do not need those services, thereby watering down the nature of preventative intervention. By contrast, our research (Compton et al., 2006) shows that five weeks of weekly progress monitoring can reduce or even eliminate the provision of preventative intervention to these "false positives"; hence, our recommendation to incorporate short-term progress monitoring in response to general education for determining students who require preventative intervention (pp. 39–40).

Example of Schoolwide Screening

JEFFERSON ELEMENTARY SCHOOL, PELLA, IOWA (SPRING 2006)

Overview and Demographics

Jefferson Elementary School has a total enrollment of five hundred students, with two sections each of kindergarten through third grade and six sections each of fourth and fifth grades. Nearly equal numbers of girls and boys attend the school. About 14 percent of the students are eligible for free or reduced lunch, and about 6.6 percent are served in special education. Five percent of the students are minority students, 95 percent are Caucasian, and six students are English language learners (ELL).

Jefferson Elementary's RTI model uses the following structure: Tier 1, Tier 2, Tier 3, Tier 4, and special education.

Screening in Reading

Kindergartners and first graders are screened using Dynamic Indicators of Basic Early Literacy Skills (DIBELS) assessments in the fall, winter, and spring. The school also uses DIBELS fluency and accuracy assessments for students in the second and third grades and Fuchs' fluency and accuracy assessments for students in the fourth and fifth grades. In addition to the fluency and accuracy measures, students in the second through fifth grades are assessed with the Iowa Test of Basic Skills (ITBS) in November and the Gates-McGinitie assessment in April. (Second graders are also given the Gates-McGinitie in October.) Jefferson Elementary also uses a variety of assessments to measure specific district benchmarks.

Screening Data and Reference Points

When analyzing students' screening data, the school uses reference points, not specific cut scores. The reference points are used to indicate whether a student is performing below expectations and to guide school staff members as they determine appropriate interventions for students. The reference points, or scores, match up with proficiency scores of standardized tests.

No single score stands alone in determining interventions for students, but rather data from multiple sources (benchmark scores, fluency screenings, DIBELS, ITBS, Gates-McGinitie) are used to determine which students need instruction beyond Tier 1 and which interventions will be most effective in meeting student needs.

Progress monitoring data also guide the determination of the effectiveness of the interventions.

Fluency Norms

Fluency norms are based on norms set by Houghton Mifflin, Jefferson's reading series. DIBELS probes are used for students in kindergarten through third grades, and Letter Sound Fluency Tests are used for students in fourth and fifth grades. To be considered to be making satisfactory progress, students at all grade levels must have 95 percent accuracy (total words correct/total words read) on the fluency probes. Charts are used to indicate words correct per minute on a one-minute timed reading.

Literacy Day Sessions and Data

The Literacy Team, which includes general and special education teachers, Reading Plus teachers, Area Educational Agency staff, the curriculum director, and the principal, meets three times a year for Literacy Day sessions. These sessions occur just after districtwide student screenings and allow team members to review the districtwide screening data as well as data from the other schoolwide screening measures. Data are then used to make necessary changes to current student interventions and to identify students who require more individualized and more intensive interventions.

For example, a Literacy Day data sheet for a fifth-grade class would include the names of the students in the left column and scores earned by each of those students on September fluency and accuracy measures and the Gates-McGinitie comprehension and vocabulary tests. A companion sheet, Literacy Day notes, would also be used during meeting discussions. Again, student names would be in the left column with adjacent columns for noting the student's areas of need, current interventions, and comments. As discussion progresses during the sessions, changes are made based on student data, students with skill deficits are considered for services, and students with extension needs are considered for gifted and talented placement.

RTI Screening Challenges

Time

Time is a big issue when conducting schoolwide screenings. Jefferson Elementary staff members have trained a group of volunteers to administer fluency and accuracy screenings to reduce the time teachers spend on assessments. They also use associates and Central College students to help in various ways.

Appropriate Screening Materials

School staff members also appreciate the challenge of determining appropriate screening materials. They agree that some choices (e.g., ITBS) are easy; more difficult to find are screening assessments to match the skills for which they want to screen. Another challenge is to acquire and use multiple sources of data to help validate skill deficits.

Data-Based Decision Making

Using the data to make appropriate decisions regarding interventions has also been a challenge for Jefferson Elementary staff. After being collected, data must be stored and sorted so they can be easily analyzed. While analyzing the data, decisions must be made about how to provide interventions to students when no current program matches their needs.

Step V

Determining How Progress Monitoring Will Be Done in an RTI Model

Question #51: What Is Progress Monitoring?

Progress monitoring is a set of assessment procedures for determining the extent to which students are benefiting from classroom instruction and for monitoring effectiveness of curriculum. A fundamental assumption of education is that students will benefit from high-quality instruction. That is, typically, students will learn and achieve the skills and content taught in the classroom. For students who are not responsive to classroom instruction, alternative interventions can be provided and again the students' response to that instruction can be monitored. Progress monitoring is a valid and efficient tool for gauging the effectiveness of instruction, determining whether instructional modifications are necessary, and providing important information for eventual classification and placement decisions.

Progress monitoring is the scientifically based practice of assessing students' academic performance on a regular basis for three purposes:

1. To determine whether children are profiting appropriately from the instructional program including the curriculum

2. To build more effective programs for the children who do not benefit; and

3. To estimate rates of student improvement

Question #52: How Can Progress Monitoring Be Useful in an RTI Context?

In an RTI paradigm, progress monitoring assists school teams in making decisions about appropriate levels of intervention (National Center on Student Progress Monitoring, 2006).

The National Association of State Directors of Special Education (NASDSE, 2005) identified nine essential characteristics for progress monitoring to be useful in an RTI context. Progress monitoring should do the following:

1. Assess the specific skills embodied in state and local academic standards.

2. Assess marker variables that have been demonstrated to lead to the ultimate instructional target.

3. Be sensitive to small increments of growth over time.

4. Be administered efficiently over short periods.

5. Be administered repeatedly (using multiple forms).

6. Result in data that can be summarized in teacher-friendly data displays.

7. Be comparable across students.

8. Be applicable for monitoring an individual student's progress over time.

9. Be relevant to development of instructional strategies and use of appropriate curriculum that addresses the area of need (pp. 25–26).

Question #53: What Role Does Progress Monitoring Play in SLDs?

Progress monitoring serves an important function in specific learning disabilities (SLDs) determination. If applied rigorously, progress monitoring addresses the federal legal stipulation that students who are determined to have a disability have not benefited from general education instruction. If the student receives high-quality instruction, progress monitoring procedures can help school staff and parents determine the extent to which the student benefited.

Question #54: How Is Progress Monitoring Accomplished in Tier 1?

In Tier 1, progress monitoring procedures serve several functions.

Progress Monitoring Versus General Screening

Proactive assessment procedures are best employed at least three times per year (beginning, middle, and end) and are used as general screening procedures for all students. Schoolwide screening and progress monitoring can serve a similar function in this regard. Screening of all students is used to determine those students who may be at risk by comparing their performance relative to a criterion measure. Progress monitoring displays individual student growth over time to determine whether the student is progressing as expected in the generally effective curriculum.

Curriculum-Based Measurement (CBM) as Primary Method of Progress Monitoring

In addition to general screening measures, a system of progress monitoring is recommended at Tier 1 for all students. CBM assesses the different skills covered in the annual curriculum in such a way that each weekly test is an alternate form. The assumption is that these alternate forms are comparable in difficulty. For example, in September, a CBM mathematics test assesses all of the computation, money, graphs/charts, and problem-solving skills to be covered during the entire year. In November and/or February and/or May, the CBM tests the annual curriculum in exactly the same way (but with different items). Therefore, scores earned at different times during the school year can be compared to determine whether a student's performance is increasing, decreasing, or staying the same (National Center on Student Progress Monitoring, 2006). If the scores are increasing, this indicates that the student's skills are improving. If the scores are remaining the same or decreasing over time, this indicates that a student is not benefiting from the intervention (instruction or curriculum) and a change is needed in the student's intervention program.

The results of progress monitoring in Tier 1 inform decision making about classroom instruction in two main ways:

1. At the class level, average performance of all students combined and their rate of growth can help a teacher or administrator determine how to create instructional and curricular change so that all students reach proficiency on the skill.

2. At the individual student level, schools use predetermined cut points to identify students in need of more extensive and intensive interventions in Tier 2 and beyond.

Question #55: How Is Progress Monitoring Accomplished in Tier 2 and Tier 3?

In Tier 2 and beyond, the purpose of progress monitoring shifts slightly. The main purpose of progress monitoring of Tier 2 and Tier 3 is to determine whether the intervention is successful in helping the student learn at an appropriate rate. Decision rules need to be created to determine when a student might no longer require Tier 2 and Tier 3 services, when a student can be returned to the general classroom (Tier 1), when the intervention needs to be changed, or when a student might be identified for special education. Timely decisions about student progress at these tiers are critical for the student's long-term achievement. The following research-based recommendations are made to facilitate timely decision making:

1. Assess student progress using CBM in Tier 2 and beyond twice per week.

2. Chart these results and analyze student progress regularly.

3. Use preset rules to determine when a student is not adequately responding to an intervention (commonly suggested rules are that four consecutive data points below the goal line warrant changes to the intervention; four above the goal line warrant raising the goal; Fuchs, Fuchs, Hintze, & Lembke, 2006; NASDSE, 2005).

Question #56: How Is Progress Monitoring Accomplished in Special Education?

In special education, progress monitoring also serves other purposes. First, the progress monitoring done to this point provides systematic, reliable, and multiple data points that can inform the eligibility determination decision and subsequent development of specially designed instruction to meet the student's individual needs. Second, progress monitoring is a requirement of the individualized education program (IEP) and provides information about student progress toward short-term objectives and annual goals.

Question #57: Will the Implementation of a Progress Monitoring System Within an RTI Model Require Shifts in School Structures?

The implementation of a progress monitoring system within an RTI model will require shifts in school structures as well as in the roles and responsibilities of educators.

Impact on Conceptualizations of SLDs

Under a system of progress monitoring, SLDs are primarily regarded as low achievement relative to classroom-peer functioning. If, for example, the bottom 25 percent of the class is selected for further progress monitoring or for placement in secondary interventions, then a student's designation for Tier 2 and Tier 3 intervention could vary depending upon what class he or she is in. The use of a dual-discrepancy model to identify students whose performance is low *and* who have low rates of progress can help remove some of this variability. Continued progress monitoring is required through the tiers to be sure that students are responsive to all tiers of instruction. If a student responds (or makes progress) in secondary or tertiary levels of intervention, the school will have to decide whether progress is great enough that the student is ready to return to Tier 1 (general education class) or whether the student should remain in the more intense instruction to maintain levels of performance comparable to peers. Students identified as in need of secondary or tertiary interventions still may require more in-depth assessment to determine appropriate instructional interventions. As progress is measured, educators obtain information about the student's level of performance and rate of gain. The measures, however, do not provide information to help educators make decisions about the student's ability or processing deficits associated with learning and performance.

School Structural Changes

General education teachers will need to consider and create (or select) appropriate assessments. These assessments will need to be consistent and similar in structure and appropriate to grade level. Another consideration is the relationship of these tools to school content and performance standards. Because best practice suggests that assessments be conducted at least on a weekly basis, teachers and schools need to develop the infrastructure to do this. A process for analyzing results at both the classroom level (to determine individual student performance) and the school level (to determine classroom performance) also will need to be developed.

Teacher Training Issues

The individual assessments and recording of information comprise a straightforward process. Many teachers already may be familiar with the concepts or be able to quickly learn and implement them after a professional development session. Teachers will need to learn to analyze results to determine which students require the next tier of intervention and when such a move should take place. Incoming teachers also will require professional development on the particulars of the school's system of progress monitoring.

Example of Progress Monitoring

CORNELL ELEMENTARY SCHOOL, DES MOINES, IOWA (SPRING 2006)

Overview and Demographics

Cornell Elementary School's enrollment consists of 440 students in preschool through third grade. Nearly 43 percent (187) of those students receive free or reduced lunch. Thirty-two students are served in special education, and five are English language learners (ELL).

Cornell Elementary's RTI model uses the following structure: Tier 1, Tier 2, Tier 3, and special education.

Progress Monitoring in the Core Curriculum

Within the core curriculum, progress monitoring is recommended if a student is new to the district and the initial assessment shows at-risk performance, if a student has previously received supplemental or intervention support and is now performing at benchmark level, or if a teacher has concerns about the amount of progress a student is making. For these students, progress is monitored weekly using DIBELS measures. School staff assess kindergartners' initial sound fluency in the fall and their phoneme segmentation fluency in the winter. For first graders, nonsense word fluency is assessed in the fall; oral reading fluency is assessed in the spring. School staff use oral reading fluency measures for second and third graders three times a year.

Core Outcomes: Next Steps

Progress monitoring in the core curriculum will be discontinued for those students who score at or above the benchmark performance level. School staff will further analyze the performance of students who score below the benchmark performance, with the goal of matching instruction to student need. These students may remain in the core curriculum with changes to instruction/practice or may be placed in core plus supplemental support.

Planning Supplemental Support

Options considered when planning supplemental support and matching students' needs with the appropriate type and intensity of resources and instruction include the following:
- More instructional or practice time
- Smaller instructional groups
- More precisely targeted instruction at the right level
- More explicit explanations
- More systematic instructional sequences
- More extensive opportunities for guided practice
- More opportunities for corrective feedback

Progress Monitoring for Core Plus Supplemental Instruction

For students who receive supplemental instruction, progress is monitored often twice each week rather than only once as with the core curriculum. School staff use DIBELS measures to assess kindergartners' initial sound fluency in the fall and their phoneme segmentation fluency in the winter. Staff members assess first graders' nonsense word fluency in the fall and oral reading fluency in the spring. For second graders, oral reading fluency is assessed; for third graders both oral reading fluency and retell fluency are assessed.

Core Plus Supplemental Outcomes: Next Steps

For students whose slope of performance is on the goal line or who are scoring at or above the benchmark performance level, two options are considered:

- A return to core instruction with progress monitoring occurring weekly
- A continuation of core plus supplemental instruction

For students who have four consecutive reading probe data points below the established goal line, who are scoring below the benchmark performance, or whose slope of performance falls below the goal line (trend line), three options are considered:

- Further analysis or assessment,
- A continuation of core plus supplemental support with changes
- core plus supplemental instruction *plus* intervention(s)

Planning Supplemental Support

Options considered when planning instructional support and interventions for struggling students include the following:

- More instructional time
- Smaller instructional groups
- More precisely targeted instruction at the right level
- More explicit explanations
- More systematic instructional sequences
- More extensive opportunities for guided practice
- More opportunities for corrective feedback

Progress Monitoring Challenges

Follow-Up Coaching and Support

For Cornell Elementary School, one of the greatest challenges continues to be ensuring the fidelity of follow-up coaching and support for supplemental and intervention-level instruction in vocabulary and comprehension.

Fidelity

An additional challenge for this school staff is ensuring continued fidelity of implementation of supplemental and intervention-level instruction over time.

Time

Finding additional instruction and practice time (core plus supplemental plus intervention) without sacrificing other core academic subjects remains a challenge.

Step VI

Understanding the Concept of a Multitiered Service-Delivery Model

Question #58: What Is a Multitiered Service-Delivery Model?

Response to intervention (RTI) is a multitiered service-delivery model. An RTI approach incorporates a multitiered model of educational service delivery in which each tier represents increasingly intense services that are associated with increasing levels of learner needs. The various tier interventions are designed to provide a set of curricular/instructional processes aimed at improving student response to instruction and student outcomes.

Much discussion continues to surround the issues of how many tiers constitute an adequate intervention (O'Connor, Tilly, Vaughn, & Marston, 2003). Most frequently, RTI is viewed as a three-tiered model, similar to those used for other service-delivery practices, such as positive behavioral support. The three-tiered model is the structure we will discuss here. Figure 6.1 depicts a three-tiered model as conceived in an RTI framework.

Like other models, RTI is meant to be applied on a schoolwide basis, in which the majority of students receive instruction in Tier 1 (the general classroom), students who are at risk for reading and other learning disabilities are identified (e.g., through schoolwide screening) for more intense support in Tier 2, and students who fail to respond to the interventions provided in Tier 2 may then be considered for specialized instruction in Tier 3.

Question #59: What is the Continuum of Intervention Support for At-Risk Students?

Figure 6.1

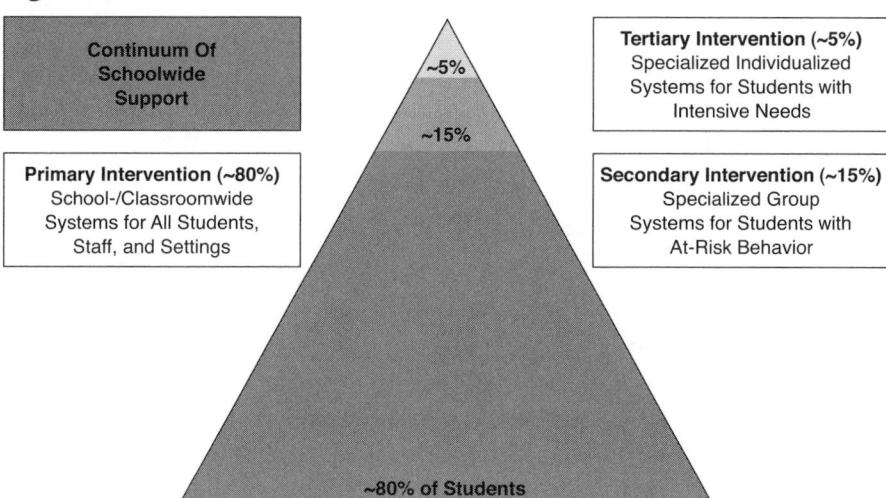

The application of RTI is typically understood within the context of a multitiered model or framework that delineates a continuum of programs and services for students with academic difficulties. Although no universally accepted model or approach currently exists, the many possible variations can be conceptualized as elaborations on or modifications of the following three-tiered model:

1. Tier 1: High quality instructional and behavioral supports are provided for all students in general education.

   - School personnel conduct universal screening of literacy skills, academics, and behavior.
   - Teachers implement a variety of research-supported teaching strategies and approaches.
   - Ongoing, curriculum-based assessment and continuous progress monitoring are used to guide high-quality instruction.
   - Students receive differentiated instruction based on data from ongoing assessments.

2. Tier 2: Students whose performance and rate of progress lag behind those of peers in their classroom, school, or district receive prevention or remediation that is more specialized within general education.

- Curriculum-based measures are used to identify which students continue to need assistance and with what specific kinds of skills.
- Collaborative problem solving is used to design and implement instructional support for students that may consist of a standard protocol or more individualized strategies and interventions.
- Identified students receive more intensive, scientific, research-based instruction targeted to their individual needs.
- Student progress is monitored frequently to determine intervention effectiveness and needed modifications.
- Systematic assessment is conducted to determine the fidelity or integrity with which instruction and interventions are implemented.
- Parents are informed and included in the planning and monitoring of their child's progress in Tier 2 specialized interventions.
- General education teachers receive support (e.g., training, consultation, direct services for students), as needed, from other qualified educators in implementing interventions and monitoring student progress.

3. Tier 3: Comprehensive evaluation is conducted by a multidisciplinary team to determine eligibility for special education and related services.

- Parents are informed of their due process rights and consent is obtained for the comprehensive evaluation needed to determine whether the student has a disability and is eligible for special education and related services.
- Evaluation uses multiple sources of assessment data, which may include data from standardized and norm-referenced measures; observations made by parents, students, and teachers; and data collected in Tiers 1 and 2.
- Intensive, systematic, specialized instruction is provided and additional RTI data are collected, as needed, in accordance with special education timelines and other mandates.

- Procedural safeguards concerning evaluations and eligibility determinations apply, as required by the Individuals with Disabilities Education Improvement Act (IDEA) of 2004 mandates.

Fuchs, Mock, Morgan, and Young (2003) used the term *standard protocol* to refer to an approach in which students with similar difficulties (e.g., problems with reading fluency) are given a research-based intervention that has been standardized and shown to be effective for students with similar difficulties and uses a standard protocol to ensure implementation integrity. The term is used in this sense in this report.

Variations on this basic framework may be illustrated by options often found within Tier 2. For example, Tier 2 might consist of two hierarchical steps, or subtiers (e.g., a teacher first collaborates with a single colleague and then, if needed, problem solves with a multidisciplinary team, creating, in effect, a four-tiered model). Alternatively, more than one type of intervention might be provided within Tier 2 (e.g., both a standard protocol and individualized planning, based on the student's apparent needs).

RTI is a critical component of a multitiered service-delivery system. The goal of such a system is to ensure that quality instruction, good teaching practices, differentiated instruction, and remedial opportunities are available in general education and that special education is provided for students with disabilities who require more specialized services than what can be provided in general education. The continuous monitoring of the adequacy of student response to instruction is particularly relevant to an RTI approach as a means of determining whether a student should move from one tier to the next by documenting that existing instruction and support are not sufficient. For example, in moving from Tier 2 to Tier 3, insufficient responsiveness to high-quality, scientific, research-based intervention may be cause to suspect that a student has a disability and should be referred for a special education evaluation. In addition, however, the right of a parent, state education agency, or a local education agency to initiate a request for an evaluation at any time is maintained in IDEA 2004.

Step VII

Determining How Problem Solving Will Be Addressed in Making Decisions

Question #60: What Is Problem Solving in RTI?

Problem solving is a decision-making process that is based on data and that is used to identify needed interventions for students in Tiers 1, 2, and 3. Decisions are made by teams that are composed of individuals who are qualified to make the important educational decisions to help students succeed in school. As a general rule, the composition of a decision-making team changes by adding additional specialists' expertise as students move from tier to tier. When using problem solving or standard treatment protocol techniques, decision-making teams should always include the student's general education teacher(s) and parents. If districts choose to use existing teams, they may need to modify procedures to align with the problem-solving steps discussed in the following section.

Question #61: Who Is Involved in the Problem-Solving Process?

Decision-making team participants may include the principal, academic specialists (Title I, English language learners [ELL], and literacy consultants), special education teachers, school psychologists, speech and language pathologists, other educational staff associates, additional general education staff, and paraeducators, in addition to parents and the general education teacher(s) of the student.

Question #62: In Making Decisions, What Type of Approach Should the Team Follow?

In making decisions, a team should use the following approach:

- **Define the problem.** When a concern is raised, the first step is to review the concern and attempt to identify the problem. The decision-making team should first review existing student data to determine specific problems. For example, a student should not be identified as simply having an academic or a behavior problem. The team should try to narrow the problem (based upon available data) to identify the deficit skill areas (e.g., phonemic awareness, problem-solving skills, math calculations, vocabulary, reading comprehension or peer interactions, etc.).

- **Analyze the cause.** Once the problem is defined, the decision-making team needs to develop a hypothesis as to why the problem is occurring and continuing. This involves analyzing those variables that can be altered through instruction in order to find an instructional solution. This includes questions of fidelity, missing skills, motivational factors, or lack of exposure to the general curriculum. The team should focus on explanations of the problem that can be addressed through instruction. In addition to the cause of the problem, the team needs to consider the student's rate of learning. In doing this, the team reviews the student's learning trend (e.g., progress) in the areas identified by the decision-making team. The team should also compare the student's progress to peers over time.

- **Develop a plan.** Once the problem has been analyzed, the team identifies interventions that will meet the student's needs. The team does this by developing a plan that includes an implementation time frame (e.g., four, six, or eight weeks), the frequency of the interventions (how often the intervention will be provided and for how many minutes per week), who will provide the intervention (e.g., classroom teacher, Title I teacher, etc.), and a time frame to evaluate the effectiveness of the intervention. The student's plan should outline the goal for progress. The team plots an "aim-line" (graphic representation) depicting the desired rate of progress a student needs to reach the goal from the current baseline.

- **Implement the plan.** Interventions must be implemented with fidelity. To ensure fidelity, qualified staff must deliver the interventions according to the prescribed process and prescribed time frame. Schools should document their delivery of the interventions using multiple sources (e.g., observation notes, lesson plans and grade books, student work reflecting instructional elements and graphs of student progress, etc.).

- **Evaluate the plan.** In order to determine if the intervention is working for a student, the team must collect data through progress monitoring. The frequency of progress monitoring depends on the tier, but in all cases, the process is similar. A student's current performance and progress is compared to their projected aim-line. If performance falls significantly below the aim-line over three or four consecutive monitoring periods, the decision-making team should revisit the intervention plan to make appropriate modifications or revisions.

Question #63: What About Using a Standard Treatment Protocol?

A standard treatment protocol is a viable alternative approach to problem solving and may be used along with, or in some cases in place of, problem solving to make decisions within an RTI system. Standard protocol is a process where student decisions are made using an established response to regular occurring circumstances.

Implementation usually involves a trial of fixed duration (e.g., nine to fifteen weeks) delivered in small groups or individually. A standard treatment protocol approach can be applied to make universal initial decisions for struggling students with similar problems. Recent research has shown that this approach can be successful when applying early interventions in reading. When students are successful in the treatment trial, they are returned to the core curriculum.

When students are unresponsive to the treatment trial, they are provided individualized instruction supported through either strategic or intensive interventions.

Standard treatment protocol may be helpful for some types of decision making early on within a multitiered system. In general, problem solving and standard treatment protocol are not exclusive and many models use both approaches. The problem-solving approach is often used more when making decisions about behavior. Standard treatment protocol often proves more successful early on in reading because it allows teams to make quick, evidenced-based decisions for a large number of students. RTI systems tend to make decisions in mathematics and writing using either approach or a combination of the standard treatment protocol and problem-solving approaches.

Step VIII

In the RTI Model Used, Determining How a Tier 1 Intervention Will Be Implemented

One concern about current approaches to specific learning disability (SLD) identification is the number of students who may actually be "instructional casualties"—those students who have not received scientific, research-based instruction in reading or other academic skill areas. Tier 1 instruction is designed to provide for the majority of students' needs and consists of three elements:

1. Research-based core instructional programs provided by the general education teacher

2. Progress monitoring of students such as through curriculum-based measurement (CBM)

3. Analysis of the progress monitoring results to determine which students are at risk and require more intense instructional support

This first level of instruction is designed to serve all students with well-supported instructional programs. General education teachers would be required to adopt evidence-based instructional programs in reading, math, and writing and to be responsible for the continual monitoring of their students' progress. Results of the progress monitoring would be reviewed periodically to determine which students were failing to make adequate progress and would qualify for Tier 2 intervention.

Question #64: What Is Tier 1 Core Instruction?

In the RTI framework, all students in Tier 1 receive high-quality, scientific, research-based instruction from general education teachers in the core curriculum. The core curriculum provides the foundation for instruction upon which all strategic and intensive interventions are formulated. While Tier 1 instruction occurs in the general education setting, it is not necessarily grade-level instruction. Instruction at Tier 1 includes all developmental domains such as behavioral and social development along with instruction in academic content areas. At this phase, general education teachers match students' prerequisite skills with course content to create an appropriate instructional match and use instructional strategies with fidelity that are evidence based.

Question #65: What Percentage of the Student Body Must Tier 1 Serve?

Tier 1 instruction must be both differentiated and culturally responsive to serve approximately 80 to 90 percent of the student body and is effective for the vast majority of students.

Question #66: What Are the Core Features of a Tier 1 Intervention?

Tier 1 includes the following features:

Size of Instructional Group

Tier 1 instruction is provided to the whole class.

Mastery Requirements of Content

Cut points identified on screening measures and continued growth as demonstrated by routine progress monitoring are indicators of content mastery.

Frequency and Focus of Screening

In general, screening assessments occur at least three times per year, are schoolwide, use a broad index, and are used to identify students who are at risk and to inform schoolwide or classwide instruction and curriculum decisions.

Frequency and Focus of Progress Monitoring

Recommendations on progress monitoring vary. In general, progress monitoring occurs at least once every three weeks and often as frequently as weekly, twice weekly, or even daily. Progress monitoring takes place in all tiers. At-risk students in Tier 1 need to be monitored at a more frequent rate than the three times per year rate provided by screening. Some researchers (e.g., L. S. Fuchs, 1989) suggest the monitoring of student progress at Tier 1 either once or twice a week. It is likely that students who receive Tier 2, Tier 3, or special education interventions will require progress to be monitored at least weekly and often more frequently. Progress monitoring assessments are focused on a class, small group, or individual student and target a specific academic skill. Results of progress monitoring provide data that can be used to make decisions about regrouping students or about continuing, revising, or changing an intervention.

Duration of the Intervention

Students remain in Tier 1 throughout the school year unless found eligible for special education and specially designed instruction that cannot be provided in the general classroom.

Frequency With Which the Intervention Is Delivered

Instruction in Tier 1 intervention occurs according to school schedules and curriculum guidelines.

Instructor Qualifications

Tier 1 instruction is provided by general educators who are "highly qualified" as defined by NCLB 2001 legislation. Tier 1 intervention is characterized by high-quality, scientifically based instruction that occurs in the general education classroom and that is implemented by the general education teacher. The use of scientifically based programs and practices ensures that student difficulties cannot be attributed to inappropriate or ineffective, poor-quality classroom instruction. Moreover, NCLB 2001 mandates the use of "scientifically validated instruction" among practitioners.

Several resources are available to assist consumers in evaluating whether an educational intervention is supported by scientifically based research. For example, the Coalition for Evidence-Based Policy (2003) advances the following three-step process in its guide *Identifying and Implementing Educational Practices Supported by Rigorous Evidence: A User Friendly Guide* to evaluate whether an educational intervention is supported by rigorous evidence:

1. Is the intervention backed by strong evidence (quality and quantity needed) of effectiveness?

2. If this intervention is not backed by "strong" evidence, is it backed by "possible" evidence of effectiveness?

3. If the answers to both of these questions are "no," one may conclude that meaningful evidence does not support the intervention.

Question #67: How Does Tier 1 Fit Within an RTI Model?

In RTI systems, Tier 1 instruction is the base level of educational service delivery aimed at meeting the needs of most students in the school setting. Accordingly, most students will achieve academic success when provided Tier 1 instruction as described in this section. Tier 1 reduces the incidence of "instructional casualties" by ensuring that students are provided high-quality instruction and monitoring.

Tier 1 is particularly important as this intervention level represents the first "gate" in a system designed to better accommodate the diverse learning needs of all students. Tier 1 provides the foundation for instruction upon which all supplementary interventions (e.g., Tier 2 and beyond, special education) are formulated in a system of response to intervention. An important benefit of Tier 1 instruction is that the high-quality instruction and monitoring highlight students who need supplemental support (e.g., small group or individualized instruction that is more intense or frequent).

Question #68: What Is Universal Screening and/or Benchmarking?

An important first step in identifying at-risk students is the use of universal screening and/or benchmarking of students in all core academic areas and behavior. Students who are at risk are not suspected as having a disability absent other data or indicators.

At Tier 1, universal screening for all students is conducted at least three times during a school year: fall, winter, and spring. Scores earned at different times during the year are used to determine whether a student's performance and progress increasing, decreasing, or staying the same. Universal screening is typically done through brief assessments such as CBMs. Significant numbers of students meeting proficiency levels (e.g., 80 percent or greater) based on the results of universal screening tools is an indicator that the instruction in the core curriculum is effective. When there is evidence that instruction in the core curriculum is not effective, schools must examine whether it is occurring schoolwide or whether it is a class specific problem. If for example a school has a high percentage of students with a particular risk factor for low achievement (e.g., low income), this does not automatically mean it is acceptable to refer a higher proportion of students in that school for special education services. Instead, consideration should be given to redesigning the core program so that it meets the needs of the school's core student population. When the core curriculum is effective, interventions within the core will need to be made for at-risk students in accordance with their individual needs based on universal screening/benchmarking data, followed by progress monitoring.

While a variety of universal screening tools are available, schools are encouraged to choose tools that are easy to administer and analyze. Schools may utilize multiple convergent sources for screening students including districtwide assessments, existing data, classroom data, CBMs, and other measurements. To ensure valid and reliable results, directions for administering screening tools and scoring the results should be explicitly followed. Teachers and staff administering and scoring screening tools should receive ongoing professional development to ensure fidelity of administration and reliability of scores. Schools should identify a standard procedure with specified criteria or benchmarks for identifying students "at risk" (e.g., create a table of cut points or patterns of performance, etc.). However, a cut score alone does not warrant movement to Tier 2 absent Tier 1 interventions that have been tried and proven unsuccessful.

Question #69: How Is Progress Monitoring Done in Tier 1?

Progress monitoring documents student growth over time to determine whether the student is progressing as expected in the core curriculum. In Tier 1, progress monitoring is recommended in addition to general screening/benchmarking measures for those at-risk students that were not performing in accordance with standards.

Analysis of the screening data and progress monitoring will expose false positives (students that appear to have skill deficits but do not) and false negatives (students that do not appear to have skill deficits but do). Unidentified, false positives result in an overidentification of students in need of strategic or intensive interventions that can be costly and time consuming. False negatives, on the other hand, can result in an under identification of students in need of Tier 2 or Tier 3 interventions.

Schools should implement screening instruments with fidelity and emphasize high sensitivity and specificity. When choosing screening instruments, greater emphasis should be placed on sensitivity to ensure identification of at-risk students. The trade-off can be increased false positives, which will later be identified through progress monitoring.

CBMs are primarily used as a method for progress monitoring and are characterized as brief, easy to administer and score, and produce measures that are good predictors of a student's academic ability. CBMs are used for both screening/benchmarking and progress monitoring.

Other measures of student performance such as classroom observations, statewide and districtwide assessments, and other standardized testing may be considered when measuring the effectiveness of the interventions provided. The data collected during progress monitoring at Tier 1 to at risk students helps teams make informed decisions at the classroom level. These data provide a picture of the student's performance and rate of growth (e.g., progress) to inform instructional and curricular changes so that every student reaches proficiency on targeted skills.

Question #70: What If Students Do Not Reach a Proficiency Level at Tier 1?

Students who do not reach a proficiency level at Tier 1 will need more strategic interventions. Lack of responsiveness is defined as the rate of improvement, or a progress slope, that is not sufficient for the student to become proficient with state standards without more interventions. Five weeks or more after progress monitoring has been initiated for at-isk students is suggested as a sufficient period to review lack of responsiveness at Tier 1. The decision to advance to Tier 2 is based upon an analysis of the progress monitoring data and a determination of a lack of responsiveness at Tier 1.

Question #71: How Will Tier 1 Interventions Affect Staff and School Structures?

Tier 1 will require significant changes to many staff roles and responsibilities and to school structures.

RTI models are intended to provide needed interventions to students in a timely manner. These models work in the context of general education and as such help ensure that students do make adequate yearly progress toward the state's learner outcomes. For many schools, this shift differs from special education as the primary service model for students with learning or performance problems. In RTI models, general education staffs have responsibility for examining student progress and achievement through a system designed to support student success and "catch" all students who experience trouble. Such a system requires an integrated approach to service delivery that includes "leadership, collaborative planning, and implementation by professionals *across* the education system" (NASDSE, 2005, p. 3). This approach represents a significant change in typical roles within the school structures. In Tier 1, general educators take a more active role in the screening, identification, and intervention processes of students judged as at risk (as evidenced by predictive screening measure results) or not meeting adequate progress (as evidenced by progress monitoring measure results).

In the RTI framework, student progress/achievement is monitored very closely—revealing a subset of students who are at risk for school failure. Some of these at-risk students will require specialized interventions within general education while others may have a disability that will be diagnosed and treated with special education. Regardless, close collaboration between general and special education will promote a more seamless system of service provision that will strengthen both the delivery of high-quality interventions for all students and the integrity of the disability identification process (Learning Disabilities Roundtable, 2002).

Step IX

In the RTI Model Used, Determining How a Tier 2 Intervention Will Be Implemented

Question #72: What Is an Intervention?

Intervention means extra help or extra instruction that is targeted specifically to skills that a student has not acquired. During intervention time, the teacher selects approaches that reach students while providing numerous opportunities for practice, feedback, and error correction. Options teachers can use to adjust the intervention include increasing time allowed for intervention, decreasing group size, changing materials or strategies, or moving students to a different group.

Question #73: What Is a Tier 2 Intervention?

Tier 2 intervention is for those students for whom Tier 1 instruction is insufficient and who are falling behind on benchmark skills and require additional instruction to achieve grade-level expectations. Although many variations of Tier 2 interventions are described in the research, in general, Tier 2 is small group supplemental instruction (ratio of up to one teacher to five students, or 1:5) provided by a specialist, tutor, or special education teacher to students who fail to make adequate progress in the general classroom. Tier 2 includes programs, strategies, and procedures designed and employed to supplement, enhance, and support Tier 1 instruction to all students.

At Tier 2, strategic interventions are provided to students who are not achieving the desired standards through the core curriculum alone. Strategic interventions supplement the instruction in the core curriculum provided in Tier 1 and should be targeted at identified student needs and stated in an intervention plan. Decisions about selecting the appropriate strategic interventions should be made when a student enters Tier 2 and then reviewed through progress monitoring at appropriate intervals after interventions are implemented.

Question #74: When Does Tier 2 Intervention Start?

Tier 2 instruction starts as soon as possible after students have been identified as falling behind grade expectations through benchmark testing. In this way, it differs from current approaches to specific learning disability (SLD) identification, in which a student must undergo a lengthy referral and evaluation system before receiving supplemental instruction. The evidence on Tier 2 interventions supports the use of a standard protocol approach, in which the supplemental instruction also is centered on evidence-based practices for students at risk. The progress of students in Tier 2 also is monitored to determine whether they are responding to the intervention.

Question #75: What Percentage of Students Need Tier 2 Interventions?

Tier 2 typically consists of 5 percent to 10 percent of the student body.

Question #76: Are Strategic Interventions In Tier 2 Short- Or Long-Term?

Strategic interventions are intended to be short-term in duration (e.g., nine- to twelve-week blocks) and are in place for immediate implementation. Interventions are generally provided in small groups of three to six students and may occur in the main classroom or in other settings. It is recommended that interventions at Tier 2 consist of three to four sessions per week at thirty to sixty minutes per session. Instruction must be provided by trained staff and supervised by individuals with expertise in the intervention chosen by the decision-making team. Students may benefit from more than one Tier 2 intervention cycle.

Schools set up and deliver strategic interventions that are designed to address routine problems exhibited by students. When selecting materials for strategic interventions, districts and schools are encouraged to identify two to three programs, or fewer, per academic area and to utilize on a districtwide or schoolwide basis for behavior. Districts or schools can identify additional programs, though limiting programs to two or three prevents redundancy and a lack of coordination across or among programs. It also reduces the amount of professional development that would be required to implement strategic interventions.

Question #77: What are the Core Features of a Tier 2 (and Beyond) Intervention?

Tier 2 and beyond consists of general education instruction plus specialized intervention that has the following features:

- **Size of instructional group.** Tier 2 and beyond instruction is provided in small groups (two to four students).
- **Mastery requirement of content.** Cut scores identified on screening measures and continued growth as demonstrated by routine progress monitoring are indicators of content mastery.
- **Frequency of progress monitoring.** Although recommendations vary, weekly to three times per week monitoring of progress is typical.
- **Duration of the intervention.** Tier 2 and beyond interventions last for nine to twelve weeks and can be repeated as needed.
- **Frequency with which the intervention is delivered.** Tier 2 and beyond provides for three to four intervention sessions per week, each lasting thirty to sixty minutes.
- **Instructor qualifications.** Instruction is conducted by trained and supervised personnel (not the classroom teacher).

Placement in and completion of Tier 2 and beyond interventions can result in one of three possible outcomes (Vaughn, 2003):

1. Successful progress is made in the area of deficit and the student exits Tier 2 and beyond instruction to return to only Tier 1 instruction.

2. Although progress is being made, the student has not progressed enough to warrant leaving and thus remains in Tier 2 and beyond for continuation of the intervention.

3. The rate and amount of progress or the level of support required for the student warrants referral for special education eligibility determination.

Question #78: How Long Should Tier 2 Interventions Be?

Although no clear consensus exists on the duration of Tier 2 interventions, in general, the research supports eight to twelve weeks for each round of intervention. At the end of this period, a decision should be made about the student's instructional needs. The options to be considered include the following:

- Return to the general education classroom if the student has made sufficient progress.
- Receive another round of Tier 2 intervention if the student is achieving progress but still remains behind his or her grade-level expectations (e.g., perhaps repeat the intervention or change to another scientific, research-based intervention depending on progress monitoring results).
- Consider for more intensive intervention in Tier 3.

Question #79: What Is a Problem-Solving Approach (Individually Designed Instructional Package)?

Most schools currently have an existing form of a problem-solving team such as a student instructional team (SIT), student study teams (SST), or building assistance team (BAT). The purpose of these teams is to develop an accommodation or modification plan for the instructional program in the general education classroom to support the targeted student, while simultaneously providing a positive effect on the instructional program for all students. Under an RTI service-delivery system, these teams would adopt a problem-solving approach that is based on data and a continuing system of evaluation. Problems need to be objectively defined, observed, and measured directly in the general education classroom. The data collected are then analyzed, using information to develop hypotheses about the cause of the problem and the appropriate selection of evidence-based strategies to remedy them. As the interventions are implemented, the student's progress is monitored at regular points in time. The team continues to meet to discuss the outcome data and determine whether the intervention is having its desired effect, whether the specific intervention needs to be revised, or whether the student should be considered for further evaluation.

Some researchers say that the research on the problem-solving approach suggests it will be used most effectively when developed and implemented according to the following attributes:

- A scientific approach to problem solving
- Interventions designed for an individual student
- A system for continual monitoring/evaluation of intervention
- Collaborative relationships with general education and special education to develop, implement, and monitor the intervention
- Collection of information from a variety of sources, including teachers, parents, and others who best know the child
- Use of curriculum-based measurement (CBM) to assist in problem identification and for continuing progress monitoring and evaluation of the effectiveness of the intervention
- Interventions embedded in the daily classroom routine so the classroom teacher takes responsibility for implementation (adapted from Kovaleski, 2003)

At this point, the evidence supporting these attributes is insufficient. Whereas problem solving has been shown to be a scientifically validated approach to help children with behavioral problems, the evidence is insufficient to show effectiveness for children with severe reading and math problems.

Question #80: What Is a Standard-Protocol Approach?

Standardized protocols are interventions that researchers have validated as effective, meaning that the experimental applications were completed with the proper experimental and control groups to demonstrate that the interventions work. School staff is expected to implement specific research-based interventions to address the student's difficulties. These interventions are not accommodations to existing curriculum; rather, they are instructional programs targeted to remediate a specific skill. Research for standard protocol interventions should specify the conditions under which the intervention has proven successful, including the number of minutes per day, the number of days per week, and the number of weeks (typically eight to twelve) required for instruction with the intervention. Information about each research-based intervention also should describe the specific skills addressed, where the instruction should be provided, who should provide the instruction, and the materials used for instruction and assessing progress (adapted from D. Fuchs, Mock, Morgan, & Young, 2003).

Many standardized protocols for reading have been developed. Some are listed in the resources section at the end of this chapter. Some of the key characteristics in a program of Tier 2 and beyond intervention include the following:

- **Focus.** The focus is on students identified with marked reading difficulties and whose response to Tier 1 efforts places them at risk for reading problems. Instruction involves specialized, scientifically based reading programs that emphasize the critical elements of beginning reading.
- **Grouping.** Instruction is provided in homogeneous small groups (teacher-to-student ratios of one-to-three, one-to-four, or one-to-five).
- **Time.** A minimum of thirty minutes of instruction per day is recommended in a small group, in addition to core reading instruction, and is generally provided over a period of eight to twelve weeks after which a determination is made about whether the student needs to continue in the program, move to more intense levels of intervention, or leave the program to receive Tier 1 instruction only.
- **Assessment.** Students in Tier 2 and beyond should have their progress monitored on a weekly basis on the targeted skill to ensure adequate progress and learning. Progress monitoring on Tier 1 skills should continue to be monitored to determine whether the intervention is resulting in improvements in reading.

- **Interventionist.** Personnel are determined by the school, but possible options are the classroom teacher, a specialized reading teacher, or an external interventionist, such as a tutor.
- **Setting.** Instruction is provided in an appropriate setting—either within or outside the classroom—designated by the school.

Question #81: How Is Progress Monitoring Done in Tier 2?

At Tier 2, progress monitoring involves reviewing existing data of the student's performance and progress using CBM tools. Progress monitoring is done more frequently at Tier 2 than Tier 1, usually occurring at least two times per month, or more frequently as determined by the decision-making team. Data gathered through Tier 2 progress monitoring informs teams of modifications needed to student intervention plans. For example, if progress monitoring data reflects student performance below the goal line over four consecutive periods of data collection, the amount and frequency of the intervention should be increased, or new strategic interventions should be added.

Question #82: What If Students Are Successful at Tier 2? What If They Are Unsuccessful?

Students who are successful at Tier 2 may be reintegrated into Tier 1. However, for a small percentage of students, Tier 2 interventions will not be enough. If a student is not meeting proficiency after it is determined that Tier 2 strategic interventions have been implemented with fidelity, the student will require intensive interventions at Tier 3.

Question #83: How Does Tier 2 (and Beyond) Fit Within an RTI Model?

We distinguish between Tier 2 and beyond interventions that might be part of an SLD determination process and a Tier 2 and beyond model used in providing early intervention for students who are at risk for failure.

In the former case, the Tier 2 and beyond interventions have an assessment role and address the assessment question of how well a student responds to a specific research-based intervention. In this role, if a student is performing at a lower level of achievement or is learning at a significantly slower rate than his or her peer group, RTI is used to determine whether inadequate instruction would account for this discrepancy.

In the latter case, Tier 2 and beyond is considered to be an intervention intended to remediate the student's deficits and promote participation in Tier 1 with general education students. Other researchers have offered a similar view of this latter purpose. Many people think of Tier 2 and beyond interventions as prereferral interventions, or "prereferral writ large" (Kavale, Holdnack, Mostert, & Schmied, 2003), that provide support to struggling students and prevent referral to special education.

Two approaches to structuring Tier 2 and beyond interventions have been described in the research literature: (1) problem solving and (2) standard treatment or intervention protocol (D. Fuchs et al., 2003). Although the two vary in their focus and implementation, the goal of each is to provide supplemental instruction to students for whom Tier 1 instruction is insufficient. Some schools may incorporate a combination of these two approaches. In some implementations, the two approaches occur sequentially with the standard intervention protocol occurring first.

Question #84: Will Tier 2 (and Beyond) Interventions Affect Staff Roles and Responsibilities, and School Structures?

Tier 2 and beyond interventions will require significant changes to many staff roles and responsibilities and to school structures. Specifically, schools will need to do the following:

- Develop or adopt an aligned system of progress monitoring and screening measures to identify the population of students as at risk or not making adequate progress in the general education curriculum and therefore eligible for Tier 2 and beyond interventions.
- Identify scientifically based interventions across the academic domains that can be implemented as intended.
- Adopt a standardized protocol (i.e., reading intervention curriculum) that is scientifically based.

- Adopt detailed procedures for consistent implementation of a standard treatment protocol or problem-solving framework for tiered intervention (D. Fuchs et al., 2003).
- Provide teacher and staff development to ensure sufficient staff to provide small group instruction.

Adopt a system for continued progress monitoring and review of results along with set criteria for exit, continuation in Tier 2 and beyond, or consideration for movement to special education levels.

Step X

In the RTI Model Used, Determining How a Tier 3 Intervention Will Be Implemented

Question #85: What Are Tier 3 Interventions?

Intensive interventions at Tier 3 are designed to accelerate a student's rate of learning by increasing the frequency and duration of individualized interventions based on targeted assessments that analyze the lack of responses to the interventions provided at Tier 1 and Tier 2. Intensive interventions at Tier 3 may either support and enhance instruction provided at Tier 1 and supported by Tier 2, or may be substituted for a portion of the Tier 1 and Tier 2 interventions if those interventions have been tried with increased frequency and duration and proven ineffective. Students at Tier 3 are those students who are performing significantly below standards and who have not adequately responded to high-quality interventions provided at Tier 1 and Tier 2.

Question #86: What Percentage of Students Need Tier 3 Interventions?

Tier 3 generally serves fewer than 5 percent of the student body.

Question #87: Are Tier 3 Interventions Short-Term or Long-Term?

Tier 3 intervention is intensive, strategic, supplemental, and often considerably longer in duration than the ten to twelve weeks of supplemental instruction provided in Tier 2. In most schools, Tier 3 might be synonymous with special education. Tier 3 is for students who fail to make sufficient progress after receiving Tier 2 interventions. In some RTI models, students who fail to make adequate progress after two rounds of Tier 2 may be referred for Tier 3 interventions. Students who receive only one round of Tier 2 intervention but whose progress is severely limited also may be referred to Tier 3.

Question #88: Who Delivers Tier 3 Interventions?

Instructional support in Tier 3 will most likely be delivered by the best qualified teacher or specialist to provide sustained, intensive support in the specified area of need. Instruction is individualized or delivered in small groups, with a ratio of no more than one teacher to three students, or 1:3. Tier 3 differs from Tier 2 in that it is more intensive instructional support, is tailored to the individual student, and may continue for much longer periods, depending on student need. In Tier 3, the student's needs are more significant, which necessitates a more intense intervention.

Question #89: Is Progress Monitoring Still a Part of Tier 3?

Progress monitoring is a continual part of Tier 3 and is used to carefully observe student response to the intervention, to report his or her progress to parents, and to determine future instructional placements. As a general guideline, a student is ready to exit the intervention when the student has reached benchmarks on the targeted skills. Students who meet targets of Tier 3 and are exited to Tier 1, but who fail to thrive without that support, also may reenter Tier 2 or, if needed, Tier 3 until they are able to maintain progress in Tier 1.

Question #90: How Are Tier 3 Interventions Delivered?

Prior to selecting intensive interventions, targeted assessments are typically conducted when a student enters Tier 3. These assessments use direct measures in addition to analysis of RTI data to provide more in-depth information about a student's instructional needs and are used to identify the student's skill deficits. Targeted assessments may be administered by reading specialists, Title I/LAP teachers, school psychologists, special education teachers, specially trained general education teachers, or other specialists. Targeted assessments include the use of interviews, observations, error analysis techniques, curriculum-based measurements (CBMs), CBM-mastery measures, which are used to target a very narrow skill, other standardized assessments, and/or functional behavioral assessments.

Question #91: What If Students Are Successful at Tier 3? What If They Are Unsuccessful?

Students who are successful at Tier 3 may be returned to previous tiers and/or the core curriculum. Students who are not successful after multiple Tier 3 intensive interventions must be considered for a referral for special education evaluation and/or other long-term planning (e.g., 504 plan, additional Tier 3 cycle, etc.).

Step XI

In the RTI Model Used, Determining When Special Education Should Be Considered

Question #92: Why Is Special Education an Integral Step in a Multitiered Model Such as RTI?

"Recent research has suggested the most productive model for improving outcomes for students with learning disabilities is one in which students' instructional gaps are identified, progress relative to the gaps is monitored, and explicit and intensive instruction provided" (Vaughn & Linan-Thompson, 2003, p. 145). A model requiring this level of intensity and individualization is typically best provided in special education.

In many schools that are organized into multitiered service-delivery systems, the tertiary tier of service may be synonymous with special education. This tertiary level of support and intervention represents an integral step in a multitiered model such as RTI, rather than a last stop or destination for a student who is experiencing school or academic problems. Special education programming and placement become necessary for the student to benefit from his or her educational experiences. As such, special education as the tertiary tier of service is intended to deliver the most intensive, scientifically based instructional programs to address individual student needs. Ideally, this tier is structured to provide flexible service, systematically permitting a student to move in and out of tertiary support as his or her needs change relative to the demands of the general education curriculum (L. S. Fuchs & D. Fuchs, 2006).

Question #93: How Does Special Education Fit Within an RTI Model?

In some RTI models, special education services are provided to students with intensive needs who are not adequately responding to high-quality interventions in Tier 1 and Tier 2 and beyond. Decisions about students' specific instructional needs are based in part on a student's lack of responsiveness to effective instruction. Eligibility decisions also are informed by individualized, comprehensive evaluations to determine the specific nature and presence of a learning disability. Special education is an individualized, iterative intervention based on data. Special education can be defined generally as specially designed instruction to meet the unique needs of students with disabilities. To achieve academic success, students with specific learning disabilities (SLDs) require intensive, iterative (recursive), explicit, scientifically based instruction that is monitored on a continuing basis (Learning Disabilities Roundtable, 2002).

Students with SLDs require a continuum of intervention options through general and special education across all grades and ages. The provision of these services can occur through accommodations, modifications, intense instruction, and remediation. Whereas accommodations and modifications are generally provided to help the student with an SLD achieve expected outcomes in the general education setting, remediation and the development of compensatory strategies are the focus of special education interventions.

A key distinction between general and special education is that special education takes an individualized approach to instruction (D. Fuchs & L. S. Fuchs, 1995). Interventions in special education must be designed to meet the specific learning and behavioral needs of the student, implemented on a timely basis, provided by a highly qualified teacher or specialist, and monitored to determine progress and achievement of desired outcomes.

In summary, the following are critical features of special education as tertiary intervention in an RTI model.

Size of Instructional Group

Special education instruction is provided to individual students or small groups.

Mastery Requirements of Content

Special education programs, strategies, and procedures are designed and employed to supplement, enhance, and support Tier 1 and Tier 2 and beyond instruction by remediation of the relevant area and development of compensatory strategies. Mastery is relative to the student's functioning and determined by individualized education program (IEP) goal setting and through results of comprehensive evaluation.

Frequency of Progress Monitoring

Continuous progress monitoring informs the teaching process.

Duration of the Intervention

Special education instruction likely will be considerably longer than the ten to twelve weeks of supplemental instruction delivered in Tier 2 and beyond.

Frequency With Which the Intervention Is Delivered

The frequency of special education instruction depends upon student need.

Instructor Qualifications

Special education teachers deliver the instruction.

Exit Criteria

Exit criteria are specified and monitored so that placement is flexible.

Specific forms of special education instruction that have been found to be most effective in teaching students with learning disabilities (LDs) combine direct instruction with strategy instruction (Swanson, 1999a). Swanson identified the main features of this model:

1. Control of task difficulty

2. Small group instruction

3. Directed questioning and response

4. Sequencing—breaking down the task

5. Drill repetition practice

6. Segmentation

7. Use of technology

8. Teacher-modeled problem solving

9. Strategy cues

The instruction and progress monitoring provided in Tier 1 and Tier 2 and beyond are an integral part of informing the intervention design and delivery within special education. The progress-monitoring results collected in Tier 1 and Tier 2 and beyond can help frame concerns about a student's progress. Special educators and related service providers will have thorough knowledge of the instruction and interventions implemented to date and can use that information to design interventions relevant to the students' learning needs. Additionally, general educators will be informed of the types of supports required in the general education classroom as students with SLDs receive accommodations, modifications, and remediation specifically designed for their individual needs.

Question #94: When Should a School District Initiate a Special Education Referral in an RTI System?

A school district should initiate a referral when it obtains information to cause it to suspect that a student has a disability or when a parent or any other person makes a referral requesting that a student be evaluated for special education services. A school district's child-find responsibilities do not end when the district chooses to implement an RTI approach. Parents, teachers, or any interested persons may also initiate a referral at any time if they believe a child requires special education services. Nonresponsiveness at Tier 3 represents a baseline within an RTI system when a disability should be suspected absent other information and school districts may not require that a student demonstrate nonresponsiveness at Tier 3 before initiating a referral.

Question #95: If a Student Is Determined Not Eligible for Special Education Services, How Long May That Student Continue to Receive the Intensive Interventions Provided at Tier 3?

Students who enter Tier 3 should initially receive at least two full attempts of intensive interventions in order to determine if they are nonresponsive. Because RTI is a system of delivering the general education curriculum, each school district determines the level of resource commitment beyond the amount of time typically needed to determine if a disability is suspected. When students are determined ineligible for special education, school districts should also consider how other federal and state funding sources can supplement implementation of Tier 3. Districts have to consider the needs of students who require accommodations under Section 504 of the Rehabilitation Act or other applicable laws. Students who have been determined ineligible for special education services but continue to insufficiently progress may be rereferred for special education.

Question #96: How Might Specially Designed Instruction (SDI) Differ From the Tier 3 Interventions a Student May Have Been Receiving Prior to Qualifying for Special Education Services?

Interventions and services a student receives once determined eligible for special education services will vary with each individual student. If a student has been unsuccessful with two attempts of Tier 3 interventions, the student's SDI may look similar to those Tier 3 interventions except the instruction will be more intense, provided with an increased frequency and duration, and adapted to meet the student's unique needs.

Question #97: Can a School District Use RTI Data to Support the Decision That a Student Has a Disability in a Special Education Disability Category Other Than SLD?

Yes. RTI data may be included when considering criteria in other categories. However, the information included in the evaluation report must be comprehensively sufficient to address each area of suspected disability. Therefore, RTI data may not be the sole source of information but may supplement information provided for suspected disabilities in categories other than SLD.

Question #98: How Will Use of the RTI Process Affect Special Education Referrals?

Individuals with Disabilities Education Act (IDEA) 2004 does not exclude or remove the use of a discrepancy model to identify students with specific learning disabilities and allows for the use of RTI data as part of the special education referral and evaluation process. Districts have the opportunity to use the rich assessment data collected by teachers from the RTI process to assist in making eligibility decisions. Final regulations to implement IDEA 2004 may clarify this process further.

Evaluation of the RTI will include information gained about student progress through the three-tier model as part of the eligibility determination for SLDs. It is expected that because students receive scientifically based instruction and focused intervention in the RTI model, the number of students inappropriately referred to special education (e.g., due to lack of high-quality instruction in reading) will decline.

Ultimately, students should be more accurately diagnosed for specific learning disabilities and the needs of those without learning disabilities will continue to be met through the core instruction and subsequent intervention instruction in Tiers 1 and 2.

The RTI process does *not* preclude a parent's or teacher's right to request a multidisciplinary evaluation for determining a student's eligibility for special education.

Question #99: What Changes Are Needed in Special Education to Staff Roles, Responsibilities, and School Structures?

Changes are needed in special education. If special education is going to lead to beneficial outcomes for the students with greatest difficulties, then teachers will need to be prepared to provide the most intensive, powerful interventions. Teachers, both entry level and experienced, will have to receive academic preparation in these methods, which will require that college and university educators are well versed and able to disseminate information about appropriate instruction and curriculum. Special education will require significant changes to many staff roles and responsibilities and to school structures:

- General and special education must be coordinated as part of a coherent system, which is held accountable for the educational outcomes of students with SLDs.
- School staff (general education, special education, administration, and related service providers) work collaboratively in planning and delivering interventions.
- A seamless system occurs when there is alignment of principles, services, assessments, preservice training, and professional development (Learning Disabilities Roundtable, 2002).

The roles and responsibilities of various staff members will depend on the methods adopted by a school or district and the available staff.

Even with general education and special education working together to ensure a seamless system of high-quality services, the ever-present questions remain:

- What is in the best interest for the student whose response to Tier 1, Tier 2 and beyond, and special education instruction is very limited?
- Does that student with such a low response receive tertiary intervention/special education instruction indefinitely?
- Should that student be returned to the more inclusive general education classroom to receive Tier 1 instruction with some supplemental special education instruction?

We do not have an answer to these questions. The literature (Bender, 2002; Tomlinson, 1999) suggests that by differentiating instruction, *all* students can benefit from instruction. IDEA 2004 specifies that schools must comply with providing a free appropriate public education (FAPE), wherein the school provides special education and related services at no cost to the child or her or his parents. We suggest that at a minimum, schools put in place procedures to document instruction and adequately monitor individual student progress in special education. For those students who are not as responsive as desired, one must carefully consider all of the options available including changes in targeted outcomes and alternative placements that could provide more intense interventions.

An Example of a Multitiered Service Delivery

ROSEWOOD ELEMENTARY SCHOOL, VERO BEACH, FLORIDA (SPRING 2006)

Overview and Demographics

Rosewood Elementary School's enrollment consists of 549 students in kindergarten through fifth grade. Each grade level comprises four or five classes. Of the total students, 165 (30 percent) are receiving free or reduced lunch, 14 are English language learners (ELLs), and 69 (including 16 gifted) are served in special education.

Rosewood Elementary's RTI model uses the following structure: Tier 1, Tier 2, Tier 3, and special education.

Core Classroom Instruction: Tier 1

The goal of Tier 1 instruction is to maximize the learning for all students using a strong research-based core curriculum to ensure that students meet grade-level standards. The general education teacher uses Harcourt Trophies for reading instruction during an uninterrupted two-hour block each day. Instruction is with the whole class and with small groups of seven to ten students each. The general education teacher assesses the students with DIBELS (kindergartners and first graders) and the Harcourt Holistic assessment (first graders through fifth graders).

In general, students in all tiers receive two hours of reading instruction each day, although the length of time spent with reading instruction varies depending on the needs of the student. In Tier 2, group size decreases and instruction is more targeted and specific. Students in Tier 3 may receive extra instructional time to address individual needs, and the staff member who provides the instruction varies. Staff members involved in Tier 3 instruction include the general education teacher, reading coach, student support specialist, elementary specialist, school psychologist, exceptional student education (ESE) teacher, and speech-language pathologist. Instruction takes place in the general education classroom.

Instruction at Tier 2

Students involved in Tier 2 instruction are those students not reaching grade-level reading standards. The goal of Tier 2 instruction is to diagnose academic concerns and systematically apply research-based, small group instruction to enable student performance to reach or exceed grade-level standards. The academic improvement plan team, which includes the general education teacher, the reading coach, and the elementary specialist, are all involved with the instruction, which takes place in the general education classroom. Instructional materials include the Harcourt Trophies Intervention Program with American Federation of Teacher's Educational Research and Dissemination "Five-Step Plan," Earobics, Road to the Code, Great Leaps, and Quick Reads. Tier 2 instruction is conducted for two hours in both whole and small group instruction. Small group size ranges from five to seven students. This instruction occurs during the same time frame as Tier 1; however, small group instruction is more targeted and specific.

Screening assessments for Tier 2 include DIBELS (kindergarten and first grade) and Harcourt Oral Reading Fluency (second through fifth grade). Diagnostic assessments for Tier 2 instruction include Fox in a Box (kindergarten through second grade) and Diagnostic Assessment of Reading (third through fifth grade). School staff monitor student progress using Harcourt Holistic assessments (first through fifth grades) and specific assessments for individual interventions.

Professional development related to Tier 1 and Tier 2 instruction is offered through district workshops scheduled for early release Wednesdays every two weeks and through Professional Learning Communities. District workshops cover the five components of balanced reading. The Professional

Learning Communities at Rosewood include the following: kindergarten—interactive writing; first grade—fluency; second grade—comprehension (author's purpose and comparison and contrast benchmarks); third grade—expository text strategies for references and research strand; fourth grade—reading comprehension (main idea); and fifth grade—comprehension targeting reference and research and main idea.

Instruction at Tier 3

Instruction in Tier 3 is focused on those students who do not respond to Tier 2 instruction, with the goal of providing intensive, individualized or small group, research-based instruction and intervention to eliminate the discrepancies between student performance and grade-level expectations. Staff members involved in Tier 3 instruction include the general education teacher, reading coach, student support specialist, elementary specialist, school psychologist, ESE teacher, and speech-language pathologist. Instruction takes place in the general education classroom for two hours a day with additional extra time as needed to address individual student needs. Tier 3 instruction is usually done one on one; small group instruction consists of groups of five students or fewer. Instructional materials include the Harcourt Trophies Intervention Program with American Federation of Teacher's Educational Research and Dissemination "Five-Step Plan," Earobics, Road to the Code, Great Leaps, and Quick Reads. Individual interventions are used to address specific areas of concern. School staff monitor progress weekly using DIBELS, AIMSweb Oral Reading Fluency, or AIMSweb MAZE.

Professional development is extensive, as described in Tiers 1 and 2, and includes Student Support Team staff development on problem solving and progress monitoring.

Instruction at Tier 4 (Special Education)

Tier 4 (special education) instruction provides sustained intensive support through a targeted curriculum for eligible students who need it to progress toward grade-level expectations. The general education teacher and the ESE teacher share responsibilities for instruction, which takes place in the general education classroom and in the ESE classroom. Instructional materials include the Harcourt Intervention

Program and Wilson Reading; these are used on an individual basis or in small groups of no more than five students. Instructional blocks of time are two hours in length and any additional time that is needed to implement instruction and interventions. Assessments include those used in other tiers plus progress monitoring using AIMSweb Oral Reading Fluency and Maze. Professional development includes all the general education offerings plus training on specific curricula and progress monitoring. Also included in the professional development activities are the following Professional Learning Communities: Behavior Management Techniques and Strategies to Enhance Academic Performance.

Decision Rules for Tier 2 and Tier 3

A student should move from Tier 1 to Tier 2 if screening assessments indicate that the student is not meeting benchmark(s), the student's classroom grades are below average, or the classroom teacher formally requests assistance. A student should leave Tier 2 and return to Tier 1 if she or he is meeting benchmarks and course work is on grade level. Tier 2 instruction generally lasts for nine weeks. However, a student may move to Tier 3 sooner if progress is not being made. This unresponsiveness is indicated by a lack of progress toward intervention goals such as three consecutive data points below the aim line.

A student should move to Tier 3 if the student shows inadequate progress with Tier 2 interventions (three data points below the aim line) but should return to Tier 2 from Tier 3 if the student has mastered the goals and can maintain the rate of progress with Tier 2 support. A student should continue with Tier 3 instruction when progress predicts grade-level performance within a year and if inadequate progress indicates a need to modify or redesign the intervention.

Decision Rules for Special Education (Tier 4)

Special education (Tier 4) should be considered when the targeted goal is not met or the student's trend line is below the aim line after implementing two or more interventions. Special education (Tier 4) also should be considered when a positive response in Tier 3 requires an intensity of resources not available in general education. State regulations continue to require ability-achievement discrepancy for eligibility.

Response to intervention data are used as evidence of educational need and for educational programming.

What Rosewood Is Learning Through Its RTI Implementation

Need to Shift From "Eligibility" to "Solving the Problem"

Rosewood staff members have learned that they need to continue the shift from making the child eligible to solving the child's learning problem. They believe that this may be best accomplished one teacher at a time.

Importance of Instructor Coaching

They have also learned that coaching is the key to faithful implementation of interventions and to teachers feeling supported.

Tiered Service-Delivery Challenges

Development of a Bank of Evidence-Based Activities

Rosewood needs to develop a "bank" of evidence-based activities to ensure quality interventions.

Finding Manpower and Resources

Rosewood needs to think "outside the box" to find the necessary manpower and resources to carry out interventions and progress monitoring.

Quest for Accommodations for Standardized Testing Versus the Model

Rosewood believes that the desire to obtain accommodations for standardized testing works against this model.

Additional Information About Specific Decision Rules

The processes used at Rosewood Elementary are the result of years of researching, learning, searching, and experimenting, and staff still do not think that they have all of the answers. RTI is a learning process, and staff members believe they are doing a better job of helping students, but they know they still have a great deal to learn.

Step XII

Determining How Parents Will Be Involved in the RTI Model

Parent involvement in a tiered service-delivery model, or any service-delivery system, should be characterized by consistent, organized, and meaningful two-way communication between school staff and parents with regard to student progress and related school activities. Through this communication, parents are enabled to play an important role in their child's education by assisting in the learning and by being involved in decision making as it affects tier-level instruction to increase their child's achievement.

Question #100: What Does IDEA State About Parental Involvement?

Parents should receive information that discusses provisions of the Individuals with Disabilities Education Improvement Act (IDEA) of 2004, noting that IDEA 2004 does not specify that their state or local school must implement an RTI model. What the law does say is that districts "may use a process that determines if the child responds to scientific, research-based intervention as part of the evaluation process" (IDEA 2004; Learning Disabilities Association of America, 2006).

Within IDEA 2004, we find the following information related to parent involvement.

Procedural Safeguards

"[E]ither a parent of a child, or a State education agency, other State agency, or local education agency may initiate a request for an initial evaluation to determine if the child is a child with a disability" (§ 614(a)(1)(B)).

Evaluations, Eligibility Determinations, Individualized Education Program, and Educational Placements

"Establishment of Procedures—Any State educational agency, State agency, or local educational agency that receives assistance under [Part B] shall establish and maintain procedures in accordance with this section to ensure that children with disabilities and their parents are guaranteed procedural safeguards with respect to the provision of a free appropriate public education by such agencies....

"[P]rocedural safeguard notices shall include a full explanation of the procedural safeguards...relating to independent educational evaluation; prior written notice; parental consent; access to educational records; the opportunity to present and resolve complaints; ...the child's placement during pendency of due process proceedings; procedures for students who are subject to placement in an interim alternative educational setting; requirements for unilateral placement...; due process hearings...; civil actions...; attorney fees." (§ 615(d)(2)(A-K)).

Question #101: What Should Parents Know About the RTI Program in Their School?

In a school setting that is implementing a tiered RTI model, parents should expect to receive information about their children's needs, the interventions that are being used, who is delivering the instruction, and the academic progress expected for their child. Frequent communication with the school, receipt of regular progress (or lack of progress) information, and participation in decision making should provide parents the information needed to determine whether their child should be referred for a special education evaluation (Learning Disabilities Association of America, 2006).

A concern often expressed by parents of students with learning disabilities (LDs) about an RTI process is whether ongoing, meaningful involvement in their child's education will depend more on their own knowledge and initiative than on school efforts. Certainly, positive home-school partnerships will depend on commitment by both parents and school personnel.

Question #102: What Questions Should Parents/ Guardians Ask About RTI in Their Schools?

In schools that are preparing to implement a tiered RTI model, parents may find it useful to pose the following questions to administrators and teachers:

- What are the provisions for including parents in the school planning process?
- What are the provisions for ensuring that parents are involved in all phases of planning the RTI interventions for their child?
- How much time must be spent in each tier to determine whether the intervention is working?
- What kinds of written materials will parents receive informing them they have the right to ask for a special education evaluation at any time?

Question #103: Are There Standards for Judging Parent Involvement?

The following provides a list of standards for judging parent involvement in a tiered service-delivery model (Mellard & McKnight, 2006):

- Standards for parent involvement are aligned with IDEA 2004 statutes (and regulations when available; e.g., due process, hearing, and placement decisions).
- Parental notification includes a description of the problem; clear, unambiguous documentation that shows the specific difficulties the child is experiencing; a written description of the specific intervention and who is delivering instruction; a clearly stated intervention goal; and a long-range time line for the plan and its implementation.
- Parents and staff reach mutual agreement on the implementation, plan, and time line.
- Parents frequently receive progress data.
- Parents are actively supported to participate at school and at home.

- Parent questionnaires and surveys assure parents that the school values their opinions.
- Parent questionnaires and surveys assure school staff that parents find school staff and school programs (e.g., interventions and instruction) to be of high quality.
- Parents view the implementation of due process procedures and protections as timely, adequate, and fair.
- School staff members strive to help parents feel welcome, important, and comfortable in the school setting.

Question #104: Are There Measures Used to Judge Parent Involvement?

The following measures can be used to judge parent involvement (Mellard & McKnight, 2006):

- Track the amount of parent-staff communication to ensure it is consistent and frequent.
- Track problem notification to ensure that it includes a clear and specific description of the problem and a written description of the intervention, the intervention goal, and the time line.
- Note practices that encourage parents to participate in their child's learning at school and at home and give them support in this effort.
- Track the opportunities given to parents to complete questionnaires and surveys about the quality of school staff and education programs.
- Note practices that make parents feel comfortable about expressing their ideas and concerns and ensure parents that their opinions are valued by school staff.
- Check that practices to keep parents well informed about due process procedures are in place and that parents find the procedures fair, timely, and adequate.

Example of Parent Involvement

DALTON GARDENS ELEMENTARY SCHOOL, DALTON GARDENS, IDAHO (SPRING 2006)

Overview and Demographics

Dalton Gardens Elementary School's enrollment consists of 411 students in kindergarten through fifth grade. Of those students, 55 percent are male. The number of classes for each grade is as follows: kindergarten—two; first grade—two; second grade—three; third grade—three; fourth grade—three; and fifth grade—two. Of the students, 19 percent are eligible for free or reduced lunch. Of the students, 93 percent are Caucasian (not Hispanic), with the remaining 7 percent being nearly equally represented by Asian, Hispanic, and African American students. Fifteen students are served in special education, and one student is an English language learner (ELL).

Dalton Gardens Elementary's RTI model uses the following structure: Tier 1, Tier 2, Tier 3, and special education.

Ensuring that Parents Feel Welcome and Comfortable in the School Setting

Parents of students with an intervention plan (I-plan) are involved from the initial I-plan meeting. Before this meeting, the classroom teacher makes the initial contact with the parents. The contact may be by phone or at a parent-teacher conference. Just before the meeting, the classroom teacher meets the parents by the school office, assists them with checking in, and gives them a brief overview of how the meeting is expected to go and who will attend. The Dalton Gardens RTI team attends these meetings. Members of the RTI team include the principal, counselor, psychologist, speech-language pathologist (if needed), general education representative (Dalton Gardens has one primary representative and one intermediate representative), special education teacher, and referring teacher.

At the beginning of the meeting, formal introductions are conducted by the meeting facilitator, usually the principal. The classroom teacher then presents information about the student to the parents and to the team members. During the meeting, team members try to be "jargon-busters" if there are terms or acronyms used that the parents may not understand.

Ensuring That Parents Are Involved in All Phases of the RTI Process and Receive Active Support for Participation at School and at Home

School staff members are aware that parents often have unique insights about their child's strengths and weaknesses and are frequently eager to help with interventions at home. When parents offer to do interventions at home with their child, the parents are noted on the I-plan as interventionists. Dalton Gardens has had parents come to the school to volunteer so they could observe the interventions in place and help with other students' interventions. Dalton Gardens staff also give parents ideas and materials that they can use at home (e.g., flash cards, reading passages with which their child can practice fluency, grammar worksheets, etc.). If a parent suggests a certain intervention, Dalton Gardens staff members are open to considering the intervention if it is something that can be provided by the staff. When parents have a suggestion, it is often something they would like to do at home.

Parents are invited to all meetings about their child, although Dalton Gardens staff members do meet without parents if they are unwilling to attend.

Parental Notification

Included in a student's I-plan is a description of the child's problem, clear and unambiguous documentation about the child's difficulties, a written description of the specific intervention(s), clearly stated intervention goal(s), and a long-range time line for the plan and its implementation. (Student time lines can vary widely.) Every nine weeks, Dalton Gardens RTI team members meet to discuss students with I-plans and to decide to discontinue the I-plan (because goals have been met), continue current interventions, change the interventions, or refer the student to special education. Parents are invited to attend these meetings.

Mutual Agreement (Parents and Staff) on the Child's Plan, Implementation, and Time Line

Dalton Gardens staff members have found that because the parents are so impressed with the RTI and I-plan process and because of the willingness of the team to do whatever it takes to help their child, parents do not have many complaints, and it is easy to reach a mutual agreement. If parents do have concerns, the school staff address them immediately and try to work with parents to make satisfactory changes.

Frequent and Consistent Parent-Staff Communication

Dalton Gardens staff inform parents about RTI through presentations at Parent-Teacher Association (PTA) meetings and through the school newsletter. At PTA meetings, school staff give a brief overview of RTI that includes basic information about RTI and the RTI process. The principal sends information about RTI to parents several times a year.

Follow-up meetings focused on student progress occur every nine weeks. If a problem comes up between meeting times, staff will call an emergency meeting to discuss the problem and the next step. The child's classroom teacher invites parents to all meetings.

Dalton Gardens Elementary distributes a survey to families each March to solicit feedback from parents about all the school programs, including RTI.

Progress Data Sent Frequently to Parents

Progress monitoring data are usually sent home weekly, if parents request it. Many parents trust that school staff will keep them informed if there is a problem. Many students who are showing good progress on their graphs ask to take a copy home to show their families.

Written Materials to Inform Parents of the Right to Ask for a Special Education Evaluation at Any Time

Parents are not given any written information formally, but during past meetings, parents have asked for testing. In these cases, the special education teacher steps in with the appropriate paperwork for parents to read and sign. If a parent asks for testing during a meeting when the special education teacher is not present and the paperwork is not available, a meeting will be scheduled for a later time to handle the paperwork necessary for proceeding with the testing. The special education teacher is very conscientious about giving parents all the paperwork and materials at the appropriate time. All staff members are willing to stop a meeting and reconvene at another time to take the appropriate steps for a student.

Step XIII

Ensuring Fidelity of Implementation

Question #105: What Is Fidelity of Implementation?

Fidelity of implementation is the delivery of instruction in the way in which it was designed to be delivered (Gresham, MacMillan, Beebe-Frankenberger, & Bocian, 2000). Fidelity must also address the integrity with which screening and progress-monitoring procedures are completed and an explicit decision-making model is followed. In an RTI model, fidelity is important at both the school level (e.g., implementation of the process) and the teacher level (e.g., implementation of instruction and progress monitoring).

Question #106: Why Is Fidelity of Implementation Important?

For valid disability determination to occur, a diagnostic team needs to be able to determine that a student has received appropriate instruction in the general education classroom. Implementing instruction with fidelity satisfies one of the IDEA 2004 legal requirements for appropriate instruction.

In making a determination of eligibility under paragraph (4)(A), a child shall not be determined to be a child with a disability if the determinant factor for such determination is? (A) lack of appropriate instruction in reading, including the essential components of reading instruction; (B) lack of instruction in math; or (C) limited English proficiency. (§ 614(b)(5))

Several studies confirm the importance of fidelity of implementation to maximize program effectiveness (e.g., Foorman & Moats, 2004; Foorman & Schatschneider, 2003; Gresham et al., 2000; Kovaleski et al., 1999; Telzrow, McNamara, & Hollinger, 2000; Vaughn, Hughes, Schumm, & Klingner, 1998).

Although these studies examined various interventions, the results suggest that positive student outcomes may be attributed to three related factors:

1. Fidelity of implementation of the process (at the school level)

2. Degree to which the selected interventions are empirically supported

3. Fidelity of intervention implementation (at the teacher level)

Although both common sense and research support the concept of fidelity of implementation to ensure an intervention's successful outcome, the practical challenges associated with achieving high levels of fidelity are well documented. Gresham et al. (2000) and Reschly and Gresham (2006) noted several factors that may reduce the fidelity of implementation of an intervention:

- **Complexity.** The more complex the intervention, the lower the fidelity because of the level of difficulty. (This factor includes time needed for instruction in the intervention).
- **Materials and resources required.** If new or substantial resources are required, they need to be readily accessible.
- **Perceived and actual effectiveness (credibility).** Even with a solid research base, if teachers believe the approach will not be effective, or if it is inconsistent with their teaching style, they will not implement it well.
- **Interventionists.** The number, expertise, and motivation of individuals who deliver the intervention are factors in the level of fidelity of implementation.

Question #107: How Can Schools Ensure Fidelity of Implementation?

When school staffs administer a standardized assessment, the assumption is that the test is administered according to the directions in the test's accompanying manual and that the examiner is qualified. Implementation of RTI must meet the same standard. Direct and frequent assessment of an *intervention* for fidelity is considered best practice. When researching the effectiveness of an intervention, it is critical to be able to report the fidelity with which it was implemented so that any resulting gains in student achievement can be accurately attributed to the intervention under scrutiny and so that the intervention may be replicated. When *implementing* an intervention, it is critical to know whether it is being implemented as designed, so that if the intervention is initially unsuccessful, schools can take appropriate measures to remedy the deficiency rather than abandoning the entire reform.

Specific proactive practices that help to ensure fidelity of implementation include the following:

- Link interventions to improved outcomes (credibility)
- Definitively describe operations, techniques, and components
- Clearly define responsibilities of specific persons
- Create a data system for measuring operations, techniques, and components
- Create a system for feedback and decision making (formative)
- Create accountability measures for noncompliance

The ultimate aim of a fidelity system is to ensure that both the school process of RTI and the classroom instruction at various tiers are implemented and delivered as intended. This aim must be balanced with the school's existing resources. General education in Tier 1, using a standard treatment protocol, is an important beginning to the RTI process. Several key components lead to high fidelity, and several key indicators are evidence of implementation with fidelity.

Question #108: What Are the Key Components and Indicators That Lead to Fidelity in General Education?

The key components that lead to RTI fidelity in general education include the following:

- Systematic curriculum
- Effective instruction
- Direct instruction
- Specified instructional materials
- Checklist of key instructional components
- Curriculum-based measure (CBM) assessments
- Videos and/or observations of classroom instruction
- Results graphed against goals
- Data (results) graphed against goals
- Student progress monitored monthly
- Decisions regarding curriculum and instruction based on data

Key Indicators

Key indicators of RTI fidelity in general education include

- 80 percent to 85 percent of students pass tests;
- improved results over time; and
- high percentage of students on trajectory (Reschly & Gresham, 2006).

Question #109: What Are the Three Dimensions That Keep Implementation of Fidelity Manageable for Schools?

Dimension One: Method

Checking the implementation of a process for fidelity can be an extremely complex and resource-intensive process. In the research literature, checks for fidelity typically involve frequent observations and recording of behavior, teacher questionnaires, and self-report or videotaping of lessons. The tools available to achieve fidelity can be divided into two main categories (Gresham, 1989):

1. **Direct assessment.** The components of an intervention are clearly specified in operational terms within a checklist based on the task analysis of the major intervention components. A qualified staff member observes the intervention and counts the occurrence of each component to determine the percentage correctly implemented and identifies those teachers needing retraining.

2. **Indirect assessment.** Included in this type of assessment are self-reports, rating scales, interviews, and permanent products. Of the indirect methods, permanent product assessment is thought to be the most reliable and accurate. Permanent products might include samples of student work or student performance on assessments and videotapes of instructional sessions.

Written instructional materials or manuals represent a necessary but not all-sufficient method of ensuring the fidelity of implementation of interventions. The use of such written materials or manuals should be corroborated by direct and indirect measures. In other words, in reviewing a checklist, a teacher might use student work samples as evidence of compliance with the outlined steps on the checklist (Reschly & Gresham, 2006).

Figure 13.1 RTI Fidelity Checklist

Student: _____   Teacher: _____

Grade:_____ Age:_____ School:_____

Features of Response to Intervention have been implemented with fidelity for the student. *Note that all areas need to be in place prior to making a referral for special education evaluation.*

Tier 1

☐ Yes ☐ No **Evidence-based general education curriculum and methodologies.** The student is placed in a general education classroom where a highly qualified teacher is using evidence-based curricula and strategies.

If yes, provide rationale and documentation:

If no, describe action step:

(Continued)

Figure 13.1 *(Continued)*

☐ Yes ☐ No **Fidelity of instruction.** The curricula including extensions was implemented with fidelity for this student.

If yes, provide rationale and documentation:

If no, describe action step:

☐ Yes ☐ No **Differentiation of instruction.** Specific instructional adjustments and/or extensions were consistently implemented to meet the student's needs.

If yes, provide rationale and documentation:

If no, describe action step:

☐ Yes ☐ No (Required fields) **Short-cycle assessment data.** Short-cycle assessment data of the student's performance in academic content areas are collected at least three times a year and compared to grade-level peers in the district. The student scores in the lowest 25 percent of his or her peer group based on this data.

If yes, provide rationale and documentation:

If no, describe action step:

Tier 2

☐ Yes ☐ No **Evidence-based interventions.** The student has received evidence-based small group instruction for at least four weeks.

If yes, provide rationale and documentation:

If no, describe action step:

☐ Yes ☐ No **Fidelity of intervention.** The intervention(s) was (were) implemented with fidelity for this student (including core curriculum, extensions, supplemental curriculum, and strategies).

If yes, provide rationale and documentation:

If no, describe action step:

☐ Yes ☐ No **Progress-monitoring data.** The student's progress was monitored with short-cycle assessment data, which was reported to parents. Short-cycle assessment data was compared to peers and the student's scores either meet the dual discrepancy or are in the lowest 10 to 15 percent of his or her grade-level peer group. Weekly curriculum-based measures (CBMs) were implemented for at least four weeks. Data from CBMs are consistent with the area(s) of concern established by the short-cycle assessment data.

If yes, provide rationale and documentation:

If no, describe action step:

☐ Yes ☐ No **Data-based decision making.** The student's individualized or small group interventions were reviewed, revised, and/or discontinued based on student performance and progress after four-week intervals.

If yes, provide rationale and documentation:

If no, describe action step:

Administrator's Signature: _____

Date: _____

Although direct assessments of an intervention are considered best practice, schools likely will have to prioritize the ways in which they plan to ensure fidelity of implementation of the various components of RTI. Many of the tools to begin a process of fidelity checks may already exist within a school or may be "built in" within the RTI process.

Dimension Two: Frequency

The frequency with which teachers are observed to ensure fidelity of implementation will vary depending upon several factors. These factors include, but are not limited to, the following:

- Teacher experience level
- Teacher requests for support
- Overall class performance
- Degree to which special education referrals do or do not decrease

In the interest of maintaining a nonpunitive viewpoint of the evaluation process, it is important that a school set up a time line for conducting teacher evaluations at the beginning of the school year.

This allows teachers to see (a) that fidelity of implementation is important to the principal, school, and district and (b) that regular observations of teachers' implementation is a typical course of action. The person who is designated as the observer (e.g., the principal or reading specialist) would ensure that all teachers are on the schedule for at least one observation.

It is important that new staff be evaluated during the first month of the school year and then further observations can be set up throughout the year depending on need. The dates for the screenings can also be included on this timeline so that teachers are aware of when the student progress data will be collected. Throughout the year, it is also important for teachers to be able to submit comments regarding the evaluation process or the curriculum as well as requests for support in the implementation process.

Dimension Three: Support Systems

As applied by schools, fidelity of implementation serves the purpose of identifying areas of deficiency that need to be remedied. For example, a newly hired teacher may not be familiar with the school's reading curriculum. This teacher might require professional development opportunities to become acquainted with the principles and procedures of the curriculum. Or a particular classroom may not have sufficient resources to implement and sustain a system of progress monitoring. This deficiency would require the subsequent attainment or redistribution of resources within the school. The kinds of support systems that are required to correct areas of deficiency likely will fall into one of two categories:

1. **Professional development and training.** This may include formal opportunities for workshops and inservice training as well as partnership with mentor teachers or coaches.

2. **Resource allocation.** If teachers do not have the proper resources to implement the intervention, it is incumbent upon the school leadership to obtain or redistribute resources.

Question #110: How Does a School Achieve High Fidelity?

Overall, a school's objective is to achieve high fidelity of implementation of the curriculum and instructional practices. If there is a high rate of fidelity in the implementation of the curriculum and appropriate instruction, this enables the administration and staff to rule out this variable with regard to student achievement. Essentially, if scientifically based curriculum and instructional practices are implemented as they were designed, then the student outcomes should be better and more consistent than previous years. When student outcomes are better, the school's instruction and curriculum program increase credibility and reliability. This credibility naturally leads to a more highly motivated staff who wish to maintain this credibility through continued faithful implementation of the curriculum and instructional practices.

Question #111: Does Fidelity of Implementation Affect School Structures and Staff's Roles, and Responsibilities?

Ensuring fidelity of implementation integrates the following three components of a school:

1. Instructional tools and strategies

2. Student achievement

3. Professional development

This integration cannot occur if teachers are threatened by the system of observation and evaluation that will accompany this process. Accountability measures related to state assessments and the No Child Left Behind (NCLB) Act of 2001 have in many cases placed an emphasis on punitive measures for teachers. We emphasize that schools should have the opportunity to implement a system of fidelity checks within a collaborative and positive environment that promotes teacher improvement. Honest and open communication with mentors or coaches can help a school tailor its professional development resources to support its staff and ultimately improve student achievement. Evaluations and observations of teachers then need to be approached in a positive manner that emphasizes problem solving.

Teacher mentors also can play a larger role in the school environment to ensure fidelity. To make this process work, mentors or coaches will need to have authority on which to act. Mentors who have proven ability in the relevant area (e.g., additional certifications, consistently high student performance, National Board Certification) should be selected to serve as coaches to new staff. Mentors may require some training for their new role, especially if they now find themselves evaluating their peers.

Step XIV

Reviewing System Requirements for Response to Intervention

Response to intervention assessment requires changes in the ways resources are used and a very close relationship between general and special education.

General educators need to understand the approach and why all of their students need to be closely monitored—especially in the development of early academic skills. Special educators must understand the limitations of traditional assessment systems and adopt highly prescribed and systematic interventions.

Most important, general and special educators need to work together to implement and maintain the system. This section details the following system requirements for RTI:

1. Leadership

2. Teaming

3. Use of a research-based, core-reading curriculum

4. Valid screening or identification procedures and decision rules

5. Adopted intervention protocols and progress monitoring

6. Policy and procedure development including special education procedures

7. Capacity building

Question #112: What Is a Leadership Team?

Moving from a discrepancy approach to RTI requires ongoing support to teams and to individuals. A leadership team at the district level will help schools move forward and sustain new practices. This team needs to be able to

- provide expertise when problems are encountered or practices are questioned;
- provide training related to learning disability (LD) identification including traditional practices and the rationale for RTI;
- identify the need for and provide support to teams with respect to research-based interventions and progress monitoring methods;
- help obtain and commit resources for screening, assessment, and interventions;
- interpret new information in the field regarding LDs;
- judge the fidelity of implementation of components of RTI and troubleshoot; and
- plan to sustain the system.

R. H. Horner, Sugai, and H. F. Horner (2000) worked extensively with schoolwide systems that address behavior supports through team processes, and they emphasized the importance of the school principal having a primary role on any such team. The philosophical and instructional leadership provided by the principal is essential to a team's ability to establish its mission, overcome difficulties, and sustain its work over time.

Question #113: What Is Teaming?

Teaming is an essential component of an RTI system. RTI requires cooperation among special education, general education, and compensatory programs such as Title I or Title III (English language learners [ELLs]). Considerations to take into account include *team membership, team structures,* and *teamwork.*

Team Membership

Experience in implementing effective behavior and instructional supports dictates that decisions about team membership be considered carefully. Generally, the team must have one or more members who

- have the authority to allocate school resources and assign work (administrative support);
- can provide leadership for the team, organize and implement agendas, and monitor role clarity and fidelity;
- are able to effect changes in the general education instructional program for groups of students (e.g., skill grouping);
- can organize and present screening data;
- are able to plan for and provide research based individualized interventions (e.g., a small group working on decoding multisyllabic words);
- can set goals for students, plan for progress monitoring, plot data, and interpret data to determine the effectiveness of interventions;
- are able to train classroom teachers and paraprofessionals to progress monitor and provide interventions; and
- represent the involvement of special education, ELL, Title, and other support programs.

Team Structures

Schools may find that more than one team best serves their needs. For example, initial data analysis and planning may be accomplished through a grade-level team. At that level, a group of teachers might find that fewer than 80 percent of their students are meeting expectations and might decide to investigate ways to strengthen their instructional program. If the core program is meeting the needs of at least 80 percent of the students, the teachers may decide to strengthen instruction for students who are marginally below expectations through skill grouping and differentiating instruction across classes. This level of the team must have measurement, progress monitoring, and administrative resources available.

Another level of the team might meet to plan interventions for students who are not making expected progress in the programs designed by the grade-level teams. This team must maintain strong ties to the general education classroom and all of the capacities listed previously.

Some schools use one central team to perform all functions of data analysis and intervention planning, at the classroom, small group, and individual level. Using a single-level team requires a substantial commitment of time and resources to both conducting the work of the team and maintaining the "health" of team functioning.

Teamwork

Teaming in order to analyze student progress using standardized data and decision making means that on occasion individuals will need to engage in curriculum or special education decisions. Successful teams establish *working agreements* about conducting meetings, decision making, interactions, and roles.

Examples of such agreements are

- team members will encourage each other to express their opinions;
- decision rules will be used to guide the team's work;
- once a decision is made, team members will support that decision;
- meetings will start and end on time;
- team members will bring necessary information to the meetings;
- the agenda will be followed;
- decisions will be made through a consensus process; and
- the principal makes final decisions about allocation of resources.

Teams should revisit their working agreements periodically to ensure that they continue to be relevant and that they are being implemented.

Planning Is Essential

As the team is formed, a yearlong plan of work should be established. There will be a cycle of reviewing schoolwide data, group intervention data, and individual intervention data that requires projecting agendas for meetings and planning to organize information to be considered.

Question #114: How Do You Use a Research-Based Core Curriculum?

IDEA 2004 requires teams to determine students not eligible for special education if their difficulties are attributed to lack of instruction in the essential components of reading instruction as identified in No Child Left Behind (phonemic awareness, alphabetic principle, fluency, vocabulary, and comprehension). Also when implementing RTI, teams must have confidence that the general core curriculum provides students with an appropriate opportunity to learn. Effective core curricula are expected to provide sufficient instruction so that at least 80 percent of students meet expectations without additional support.

Reading is set apart as especially important because the majority of students with learning disabilities are identified with problems learning to read. Other academic areas are substantiated with less research, but curricula and instruction may be validated by meeting these guidelines:

1. The curriculum that is being used has been analyzed and is aligned with benchmarks.

2. Instruction is intense, regular, and differentiated to meet the skill needs of individual students.

3. At least 80 percent of students are meeting expectations such as benchmarks.

It is particularly important to examine the "80 percent" criterion. This expectation is a general guideline, and teams should adjust that expectation to a higher level if the general achievement in the school is typically higher than 80 percent. In some schools, the expectation is more appropriately 85 percent or even 90 percent. Performance in each classroom is expected to be close to the school average.

While the criterion may be adjusted upward, it should not be adjusted downward.

It should be assumed that, if 80 percent of students in a district, school, or classroom are not meeting benchmarks, the problem is with either the content of the core curriculum or the intensity and frequency of instruction.

Question #115: What Are Valid Screening or Identification Procedures and Decision Rules?

School personnel need to know when a student is at risk of failure in a core academic subject. Whether a district adopts a problem-solving, prereferral, or tiered model of RTI, teachers or teams need to know when to select a student for intervention. This requires that valid data are examined on a regular schedule and that students are selected for intervention on this basis. Data that may inform these decisions include:

1. Dynamic Indicators of Basic Early Literacy Skills (DIBELS);

2. curriculum-based measures (CBMs);

3. fluency measures with norms that are local or based on national studies;

4. statewide assessments;

5. locally developed measures that can be interpreted on consistent, objective criteria;

6. behavior and attendance data that can be interpreted on consistent, objective criteria; and

7. teacher concern.

Using clearly defined criteria and decision rules—for example, "Students who are in the lowest 10 percent of the class will be selected for interventions"—helps to teachers' level of tolerance with respect to students who are struggling. These decision rules are those that are used to select students for intervention.

Decision rules are also necessary to ensure that students who are not responding adequately move to more intensive or appropriate interventions and that a decision is made to complete the special education referral process when needed. An example of this kind of decision rule is "change the intervention when the student does not meet the aim line for three consecutive data points." These types of rules are those that govern the intervention process.

Question #116: What Are Adopted Intervention Protocols and Progress Monitoring Intervention Protocols?

There is some concern that RTI-based decisions will lack uniformity. This concern is based at least partially on the difficulty in documenting what interventions have been provided and their levels of intensity and duration.

Those concerns may be addressed by carefully standardizing interventions.

Gresham (2002) reviewed research in reading interventions and determined that a combination of direct instruction and strategy instruction produces the greatest effects for struggling students. Other authorities (National Reading Panel, 2000; Shaywitz, 2004) add fluency instruction as an important component of interventions for many students.

Interventions become increasingly intense as students do not respond adequately. Intensity is achieved by changing group size, expertise of the teacher, duration or frequency of lessons, or motivation.

As interventions become more intense, it is difficult to provide both general education curriculum *and* interventions to a student. It is recommended that when there simply is not enough time in the school day to provide an intensive intervention, programming like extended school day be considered. Another approach is to provide the systematic basic skills instruction and practice in the intervention setting and include students in language and comprehension instruction in the general education classroom. For example, in math the student would be included in the general education classroom for conceptual, vocabulary, and math reasoning instruction. A menu of interventions should be developed that match area of deficit, curricula, and intensity to specific student profiles.

The following steps may be used in designing an intervention:

1. Identify students with similar skill deficits (e.g., math fact fluency).

2. Specify each child's deficit level (e.g., writes ten correct facts per minute).

3. Identify a curriculum that is specific to the skill deficit(s).

4. Identify an instructor who has been trained to use the curriculum.

5. Decide how long the intervention will progress before review.

6. Develop a progress monitoring chart for each student that includes a clearly marked benchmark and aim line.

Progress Monitoring

Progress monitoring is assessment of students' academic performance on a regular basis in order to determine whether children are benefiting from instruction and to build more effective programs for those who are not. Standard methods of progress monitoring prevent inconsistency in decision making and eligibility decisions. Progress monitoring for these purposes must include clear benchmarks for performance and reliable, easy to administer measures such as curriculum-based measures (CBMs).

Progress monitoring involves the following steps:

1. Establish a benchmark for performance and plot it on a chart (e.g., "read orally at grade level, forty words per minute by

June"). It must be plotted at the projected end of the instructional period, such as the end of the school year.

2. Establish the student's current level of performance (e.g., "twenty words per minute").

3. Draw an aim line from the student's current level to the performance benchmark. This is a picture of the slope of progress required to meet the benchmark.

4. Monitor the student's progress at equal intervals (e.g., every third instructional day). Plot the data.

5. Analyze the data on a regular basis, applying decision rules (e.g., "the intervention will be changed after three data points that are below the aim line").

6. Draw a trend line to validate that the student's progress is adequate to meet the goal over time.

Question #117: What Are Policy and Procedure Developments Including Special Education Procedures?

Adopting RTI

RTI is a system that affects both general and special education. Districts that have successfully implemented these approaches experience substantial systemwide benefits for all children. However, obtaining "buy-in" and cooperation for use of resources is essential. Administrative support from the top down and teacher support from the bottom up are vital to success and sustainability.

Initially, RTI will require extra resources for training and time for teams to work together. Support services such as ELL and Title I may need to be reorganized.

Funds may need to be set aside to provide interventions. Commitment and planning need to be in place before RTI is implemented. IDEA 2004 offers districts the opportunity to support the RTI process by using IDEA funds for "early intervening services." These coordinated services are preventative in nature and function within the general education context.

Defining and Adopting Procedures

When moving to an RTI approach, a set of fluid activities (data review, intervention implementation, and analysis) are used much like we have used traditional testing instruments. These activities may be difficult for some teams to track. Individuals must conduct those activities in standardized ways, documenting their work, and using standardized decision-making guidelines. This prevents arbitrary decision making and ensures that students move through the system and that they are considered for evaluation and eligibility in a timely manner.

Decision Rules

This essential procedural component has been referenced several times. An example of decision rules used by the Effective Behavior and Instructional Support (EBIS; Sadler, 2002) are

1. organize the lowest 20 percent of students in the group (class, grade level, or school) to receive interventions;

2. students in group interventions are monitored weekly;

3. students in individual interventions are monitored at least once weekly;

4. change interventions when three consecutive data points do not meet the student's goal line;

5. move students to an individual intervention after two unsuccessful group interventions; and

6. refer a student for special education after one unsuccessful individual intervention.

Parental Notice and Consent

Procedures must clearly establish when and how parents are involved in the RTI process. Questions to answer ahead of time include the following: "When are parents invited to team meetings?" "When are parents provided with procedural safeguards?" "When is parental consent required?" In the EBIS system, parents are notified of any individual intervention. Since it has been found that a second individual intervention is typically provided to students who are or will be referred for special education, it is at this point a special education referral is made and consent for evaluation is obtained.

Special Education Procedures

As described in the general section on RTI, all of the evaluation requirements for special education remain in effect when implementing this approach. This means that teams need to be very clear about an evaluation planning process that regards the use of response to intervention as one component of a full and individual evaluation. Districts need to develop well-defined procedures and ensure teams are trained before implementing RTI.

Evaluation Planning and Eligibility Determination

Using an RTI model to decide whether a student has an LD involves systematic application of professional judgment. Through the review of data obtained from multiple sources, consideration of those data within specific contexts, and thoughtful discourse, a team is prepared to make an eligibility decision. More complex than relying on a simple numerical formula, this process produces decisions that reflect the benefit of collective knowledge, expertise, and insight of the team.

Question #118: What Is Capacity Building?

It is imperative that a core group of district staff deeply understands current research on the identification of learning disabilities. The leadership team referred to earlier might serve to teach broader groups of teachers, specialists, and administrators. This team will need time to study and master issues around LD identification, reading instruction, and progress monitoring.

Special educators must grasp the foundational underpinnings of RTI and the research from which they developed. Additionally, this group of staff will need training specifically targeting the transition from a discrepancy model to RTI—why is practice changing? This group's level of understanding must be sufficient to support implementation of the RTI approach as well as explaining the approach to colleagues and parents. Many practitioners will need to review and discuss this information several times before they are comfortable with the core concepts.

General educators require training on the same topics, though understanding need not be as comprehensive. The focus of training for this group is on the importance of early skill development and monitoring of that development, the redefined view of general education as providing first level interventions, and the need for collaboration.

For some team members, this will require a fundamental change in the way part of their job is accomplished. For example, when IQ testing is not a routine part of each LD evaluation, school psychologists will play a very different role on a team. Their time may be used to conduct more targeted evaluations of attention or behavioral characteristics, consultation, or to assist with additional progress monitoring.

Where teaming is not a norm, deliberate planning for team formation and functioning is required. When a group is adopting both new practices and new ways of doing work, individuals may experience significant stress. A professional facilitator can help a team define its mission, establish norms, and improve skills like conflict management and negotiation.

Conclusion

RTI models have the capacity to improve outcomes for and provide support to students who are both low achieving and who have learning disabilities (LDs). They do, however, require substantial cooperation between regular and special education. They also require that procedures be used within general education to impact the general education curriculum and teacher practices. Widespread progress monitoring of all students, systematic intervening within general education, and collegial problem solving are hallmarks of RTI.

New Roles for Professionals in Education

For all education professionals, the new instruction, assessment, documentation, and collaborative activities required for RTI implementation will create new challenges.

The following are examples:

1. General education teachers will need to compile relevant assessment data through continuous progress monitoring and respond appropriately to the findings.

2. Special education, pupil personnel, related services, and other support professionals (e.g., special education teachers, speech-language pathologists, school psychologists, reading specialists, educational therapists, occupational and physical therapists, and audiologists) need to help design, interpret, and assess data as well as suggest instructional approaches.

3. Specialists including special education teachers and LD specialists providing more intensive interventions will be

expected to master a variety of scientific, research-based methods and materials, and provide them with fidelity to groups of various sizes in different environments.

4. Administrative and supervisory staff will have to determine needed roles and competencies, existing skill levels, and professional development requirements in order to provide immediate and ongoing training activities in these critical areas.

5. Critical questions also will arise about how a particular RTI approach will affect the specific roles and competencies required of education professionals. Decisions about these roles and resulting needed competencies include the following:

- Who is to deliver and monitor the high-quality instruction needed in the various settings of RTI?
- Who will schedule and determine the composition of each decision-making team?
- Who will manage and supervise placement, services, and follow-up activities?
- Who will have formal responsibility for ensuring that all professionals involved in an RTI approach possess the specific needed competencies and attitudes?
- Who will ensure ongoing involvement of and approval by parents?

In some cases, the answers to such questions may influence an RTI approach adopted, suggest needed adaptations, prompt professional development efforts, or result in delay, scaling back, or abandonment of a specific RTI approach. Answers to these questions may lead to additional questions such as (a) are there competencies unique to successful teaching of students with LDs, (b) how can the needed competencies be developed in novice and experienced professionals, and (c) which competencies best match the roles and competencies of RTI models?

New Competencies in Professional Educators

Competencies in LD

Effective implementation of RTI requires new roles for school personnel who serve students with LDs. There may be an overlap between the competencies required of special education, general education, and related service providers. Uncertainty exists about the levels of competence required for fulfilling the diagnostic, instructional, collaborative, and consultative roles expected of personnel who serve students with LDs. For example, an RTI approach will require that (a) general education teachers provide evidence-based, differentiated instruction, continuous data monitoring, and timely identification of nonresponsive students; and (b) the general education teacher or specialist will provide individualized, more intensive instruction for nonresponsive students in one of several settings. These two examples suggest that schools will need a staff with a wide range of competencies.

Other Factors Affecting Competency

One of the most fundamental questions about ensuring competence in teachers and related service professionals focuses on the skills critical for beginning professionals, in contrast to those expected of experienced, but perhaps less up to date, practicing professionals. Most seem to agree that field experiences and mentoring are vital to the success and retention of beginning professionals. Similarly, there is general agreement that recent instructional research, especially in early decoding skills needed for reading, must be integrated into the practice of both beginning and practicing teachers. Less evident but equally important are collaborative skills for all personnel. In school cultures that treat general education and special education as separate, it may be difficult to develop the interdependence expected in an RTI approach. Strategic planning and staff development will be needed to address all of these factors and support the successful implementation of RTI.

Documenting Competencies and Qualifications

The impact of factors such as state licensure, higher education accreditation, certification routes, private agency training, and the requirements of No Child Left Behind Act (NCLB) and Individuals with Disabilities Education Act (IDEA) 2004 will be important considerations if the needed competencies are to be internalized and applied in practice with individual students in the range of RTI settings.

The most common way to recognize qualifications and competence in the professions including teaching is documentation from a recognized state agency or professional organization. State certification or licensure by a state is generally considered evidence of competence in the area for which it is received. More recently, other routes have become available such as alternate certification, the National Board for Professional Teaching Standards certification, certificates from nonprofit organizations, and formal recognition from a variety of other entities that acknowledge training and/or experience. Each of these provides potential routes for documentation of competencies needed to contribute effectively within an RTI approach.

Recruitment and Retention of Qualified Personnel

A critical problem is ensuring the availability of highly qualified teachers to provide effective instruction, intervention, and collaboration. Whether the new responsibilities of an RTI approach, especially when successful, will motivate teachers to stay in classrooms (i.e., if it acts as a career ladder) is an empirical question.

IDEA 2004 anticipates the resource requirements of such an approach, allowing for use of up to 15 percent of Part B funds for "early intervening" services for students who are not yet identified as having a disability. Districts can both adopt a new diagnostic approach and benefit children before their low performance becomes an intractable achievement deficit that may be accompanied by low motivation and behavioral problems. However, districts must carefully determine which model of RTI is most appropriate within their system and implement standardized procedures aligned to state criteria.

Schools are already encumbered by numerous policy initiatives, increasingly diverse student needs, and limited resources. RTI has the potential to help a school make better use of its resources for increasing overall student achievement and for serving students with learning disabilities by

- allowing for early identification of at-risk students;
- aligning assessment procedures with instruction;
- providing multiple data points on which decisions are based; and
- ensuring access to appropriate instruction through the use of progress monitoring and evidence-based instruction.

While there is a pressing need for research and evaluation data about RTI, it is an enormously complex undertaking. The need for evaluating the implementation of RTI in actual practice, particularly in large-scale applications, is paramount. However, it is important to acknowledge that the outcomes of RTI implementation will vary on a number of key factors such as selection and fidelity of interventions, decisions about time frames, criteria for movement among tiers, resources, and staff training. These and other key factors will affect generalization and replication of results. Strict adherence to meeting established research standards is critical for informing instruction and vital for improving the academic outcomes and life success for students with LDs.

However, these potentials cannot be realized if screening procedures, interventions, and progress monitoring procedures are not properly implemented. Initially, ensuring fidelity will be a fairly resource-intensive process; it will continue to require resources as schools receive new staff and students. We have described a framework and the tools and procedures that schools can use to develop a system of ensuring fidelity that supports but does not overwhelm schools as they implement RTI.

References

Bender, W. N. (2002). *Differentiating instruction for students with learning disabilities: Best teaching practices for general and special educators.* Thousand Oaks, CA: Corwin Press.

Caplan, G., & Grunebaum, H. (1967). Perspectives on primary prevention: A review. *Arch Gen Psychiatry, 17,* 331–346.

Coalition for Evidence-Based Policy. (2003). *Identifying and implementing educational practices supported by rigorous evidence: A user friendly guide.* Washington, DC: Author. Retrieved March 15, 2006, from http://www.ed.gov/rschstat/research/pubs/rigorousevid/rigorousevid.pdf.

Deno, S., Grimes, J., Reschly, D., & Schrag, J. (2001). PSM review team report. Minneapolis: Minneapolis Public Schools.

Division for Learning Disabilities of the Council for Exceptional Children (2006). Teaching students with learning disabilities. Retrieved on August 30, 2007, from www.teachingld.org

Drame, E. R. (2002). Sociocultural context effects on teacher's readiness to refer for learning disabilities. *Council for Exceptional Children, 69*(1), 41–53.

Fletcher, J. M., Francis, D. J., Shaywitz, S. E., Lyon, G. R., Foorman, B. R., Steubing, K. K., et al. (1998). Intelligent testing and the discrepancy model for children with learning disabilities. *Learning Disabilities Research and Practice, 13*(4), 186–203.

Fletcher, J. M., Lyon, G. R., Barnes, M., Steubing, K. K. Francis, D. J., Olson, R. K., et al. (2002). Classification of learning disabilities: An evidence-based evaluation. In R. Bradley, L. Danielson, & D. P. Hallahan (Eds.), *Identification of learning disabilities: Research to practice.* Mahwah, NJ: Lawrence Erlbaum Associates.

Foorman, B. R., & Moats, L. C. (2004). Conditions for sustaining research-based practices in early reading instruction. *Remedial and Special Education, 25*(1), 51–60.

Foorman, B. R., & Schatschneider, C. (2003). Measuring teaching practices in reading/language arts instruction and their relation to student achievement. In S. Vaughn and K. Briggs (Eds.), *Reading in the classroom: Systems for observing teaching and learning.* Baltimore, MD: Brookes Publishing Co.

Francis, D. J., Fletcher, J. M., Stuebing, K. K., Lyon, G. R., Shaywitz, B. A., & Shaywitz, S. E. (2005). Psychometric approaches to the identification of LD: IQ and achievement scores are not sufficient. *Journal of Learning Disabilities, 38*(2), 98–108.

Fuchs, D., & Fuchs, L. S. (1995). What's "special" about special education? *Phi Delta Kappan, 76*(7), 522–530.

Fuchs, D., Fuchs, L., Hintze, J., & Lembke, E. (2006). *Using curriculum-based measurement to determine response to intervention.* Retrieved April 13, 2007, from http://www.studentprogress.org/summer_institute/inst2006.asp

Fuchs, D., Fuchs, L. S., Hintze, J., & Lembke, E. (2006, July). Progress monitoring in the context of response-to-intervention. Presentation at the Summer Institute on Student Progress Monitoring, Kansas City, MO.

Fuchs, D., Mock, D., Morgan, P. L., & Young, C. L. (2003). Response-to-intervention: Definitions, evidence, and implications for the learning disabilities construct. *Learning Disabilities Research and Practice, 18*(3), 157–171. Fuchs, L. S., Fuchs, D., & Speece, D. L. (2002). Treatment validity as a unifying construct for identifying learning disabilities. Learning Disability Quarterly, 25, 33–45.

Fuchs, L. S. (1989). Evaluating solutions: Monitoring progress and revising intervention plans. In M. R. Shinn (Ed.), *Curriculum-based measurement: Assessing special children* (pp. 153–181). New York: Guilford Press.

Fuchs, L. S., & Fuchs, D. (1998). Treatment validity: A unifying concept for reconceptualizing the identification of learning disabilities. *Learning Disabilities Research & Practice, 13*(4), 204–219.

Fuchs, L. S., & Fuchs, D. (2006). Implementing response-to-intervention to identify learning disabilities. *Perspectives on Dyslexia, 32*(1), 39–43.

Gerber, M. M., & Semmel, M. I. (1984). Teacher as imperfect test: Reconceptualizing the referral process. *Educational Psychologist, 19*, 1–12.

Good, R. H., & Kaminski, R. A. (Eds.). (2002). *Dynamic Indicators of Basic Early Literacy Skills* (6th ed.). Eugene, OR: Institute for the Development of Education Achievement.

Gresham, F. M. (1989). Assessment of treatment integrity in school consultation and prereferral intervention. *School Psychology Review, 18*(1), 37–50.

Gresham, F. M. (2002). Response to intervention: An alternative approach to the identification of learning disabilities. In R. Bradley, L. Danielson, & D. P. Hallahan (Eds.), *Identification of learning disabilities: Research to practice.* Mahwah, NJ: Lawrence Erlbaum Associates. [AU NOTE: Please supply page numbers.]

Gresham, F. M., MacMillan, D., & Bocian, K. (1997). Teachers as "tests": Differential validity of teacher judgments in identifying students at-risk for learning difficulties. *School Psychology Review, 26*, 47–60.

Gresham, F. M., MacMillan, D. L., Beebe-Frankenberger, M. E., & Bocian, K. M. (2000). Treatment integrity in learning disabilities intervention research: Do we really know how treatments are implemented? *Learning Disabilities Research & Practice, 15*(4), 198–205.

Hallahan, D. P., & Mercer, C. D. (2002). Learning disabilities: Historical perspectives. In R. Bradley, L. Danielson, & D. P. Hallahan (Eds.),

Identification of learning disabilities: Research to practice. Mahwah, NJ: Lawrence Erlbaum Associates.

Horner, R. H., Sugai G., & Horner, H. F. (2000). A school-wide approach to student discipline. *The School Administrator, 2*(57), 20–23.

Howell, K. W., & Nolet, V. (2000). *Curriculum-based evaluation: Teaching and decision-making* (3rd ed.). Belmont, CA: Wadsworth/Thomson Learning.

Huitt, W. (1996). Summary of principles of direct instruction: Educational psychology interactive. Valdosta, GA: Valdosta State University. Retrieved July 6, 2005, from http://chiron.valdosta.edu/whuitt/col/instruct/dirprn.html

Ikeda, M. J., & Gustafson, J. K. (2002). Heartland AEA 11's problem solving process: Impact on issues related to special education (Research Rep. No. 2002-01). Johnston, IA: Heartland Area Education Agency.

Individuals with Disabilities Education Improvement Act of 2004. (Public Law 108-446).

Jenkins, J. R. (2003, December). *Candidate measures for screening at-risk students.* Paper presented at the NRCLD Response to Intervention Symposium, Kansas City, MO. Retrieved April 3, 2006, from http://www.nrcld.org/symposium2003/jenkins/index.html

Johnson, E., Mellard, D., Fuchs, D., & McKnight, M. (2006). *Response to intervention (RTI): How to do it.* Lawrence, KS: National Research Center on Learning Disabilities.

Kame'enui, E. J., & Simmons, D. C. (2002). From an "exploded view" of beginning reading toward a schoolwide beginning reading model: Getting to scale in complex host environments. In R. Bradley, L. Danielson, & G. R. Lyon (Eds.), *Learning disabilities and early intervention strategies: How to reform the special education referral and identification process: Hearing before the Committee on Education and the Workforce.* Retrieved August 3, 2005, from http://edworkforce.house.gov/hearings/107th/edr/idea6602/lyon.htm

Kavale, K. A., Holdnack, J., Mostert, M. P., & Schmied, C. M. (2003, December). *The feasibility of a response to intervention approach for the identification of specific learning disability: A psychometric alternative.* Paper presented at the NRCLD Response to Intervention Symposium, Kansas City, MO. Retrieved March 15, 2006, from http://www.nrcld.org/symposium2003/kavale/index.html

Kovaleski, J. F. (2003, December). *The three tier model for identifying learning disabilities: Critical program features and system issues.* Paper presented at the NRCLD Response to Intervention Symposium, Kansas City, MO. Retrieved March 15, 2006, from http://www.nrcld.org/symposium2003/kovaleski/index.html

Kovaleski, J. F., Gickling, E. E., & Marrow, H. (1999). High versus low implementation of instructional support teams: A case for maintaining program fidelity. Remedial and Special Education, 20, 170–183.

Learning Disabilities Association of America. (2006). *Information on response to intervention.* Pittsburgh, PA: Author. Retrieved March 15, 2006, from http://www.ldaamerica.org/

Learning Disabilities Roundtable. (2002, July). *Specific learning disabilities: Finding common ground: A report by the ten organizations participating in the*

Learning Disabilities Roundtable, sponsored by the Division of Research, Office of Special Education Programs, Department of Education. Washington, DC: Author. Retrieved April 11, 2006, from http://www.ncld.org/content/view/280

Learning Disabilities Roundtable. (2005, February). *Comments and recommendations on regulatory issues under the Individuals with Disabilities Education Improvement Act of 2004 (Public Law 108-446).* Washington, DC: Author.

Lemon, M. (2005). IDEA '04 requires new special education practices. Retrieved on October 9, 2007 from: http://www.obkcg.com/article.asp?a=126

Lyon, G. R., Fletcher, J. M., Shaywitz, S. E., Shaywitz, B. A., Torgeson, J. K., Wood, F. B., et al. (2001). Rethinking learning disabilities. In C. E. Finn Jr., A. J. Rotherham, & C. R. Hokanson Jr. (Eds.), *Rethinking special education for a new century* (pp. 259–287). Washington, DC: Progressive Policy Institute and the Thomas B. Fordham Foundation.

Marston, D. (2001, August). A functional and intervention-based assessment approach to establishing discrepancy for students with learning disabilities. Paper presented at the LD Summit, Washington, DC.

Marston, D. (2003, December). *Comments on three papers addressing the question: "How many tiers are needed within RTI to achieve acceptable prevention outcomes and to achieve acceptable patterns of LD identification?"* Paper presented at the NRCLD Response to Intervention Symposium, Kansas City, MO. Retrieved March 15, 2006, from http://www.nrcld.org/symposium 2003/marston/index.html

Marston, D., Canter, A., Lau, M., & Muyskens, P. (2002, June). Problem solving: Implementation and evaluation in Minneapolis schools. *NASP Communiqué, 30*(8). Retrieved July 21, 2005, from http://www.naspon line.org/publications/cq308minneapolis.html

Marston, D., Muyskens, P., Lau, M., & Canter, A. (2003). Problem-solving model for decision making with high-incidence disabilities: The Minneapolis experience. Learning Disabilities: Research and Practice, 18(3), 187–200.

McGrady, H. J. (2002). A commentary on "empirical and theoretical support for direct diagnosis of learning disabilities by assessment of intrinsic processing weaknesses." In R. Bradley, L. Danielson, & D. P. Hallahan (Eds.), Identification of learning disabilities: Research to practice. Mahwah, NJ: Lawrence Erlbaum Associates.

Mellard, D. F., & McKnight, M. A. (2006). *RTI implementation tool for reading: Best practices.* Lawrence, KS: National Research Center on Learning Disabilities.

National Association of State Directors of Special Education. (2005). *Response to Intervention: Policy considerations and implementation.* Alexandria, VA: Author.

National Center on Student Progress Monitoring, (2006). *Response to intervention.* Retrieved on March 13, 2007, from http://www.student progress.org/news/default.asp

National Joint Committee on Learning Disabilities. (2005). *Response to intervention and learning disabilities.* Retrieved on July 23, 2007, from http://www.nasponline.org/advocacy/RTI%20Final%20August%2020 05.pdf

National Reading Panel. (2000). *Teaching children to read: An evidence-based assessment of the scientific research literature on reading and its implications for reading instruction.* Washington, DC: National Institutes of Health.

National Research Center on Learning Disabilities. (2006). Understanding response to intervention in learning disabilities determination. Retrieved from http://www.nrcld.org

National Research Council. (2002). *Scientific research in education.* Washington, DC: National Academy Press.

No Child Left Behind Act of 2001. (Public Law 107-110).

O'Connor, R., Tilly, D., Vaughn, S., & Marston, D. (2003). *Session 5: How many tiers are needed within RTI to achieve acceptable prevention outcomes and to achieve acceptable patterns of LD identification?* Paper presented at NRCLD Symposium, Response to Intervention, Kansas City, MO. Retrieved from http://www.nrcld.org/symposium2003/index.html Retrieved on April 30, 2007.

President's Commission on Excellence in Special Education. (2002). *A new era: Revitalizing special education for children and their families.* Jessup, MD: ED Pubs, Education Publications Center, U.S. Department of Education. Retrieved October 18, 2007 from http://www.ed.gov/inits/commissions boards/whspecialeducation/reports/index.html

Pressley, M. (2000). Comprehension instruction: What makes sense now, what might make sense soon. In M. L. Kamil, P. B. Mosenthal, P. D. Pearson, & R. Barr (Eds.), *Handbook of reading research* (Vol. 3). Mahwah, NJ: Lawrence Erlbaum Associates.

Reschly, D. J., (2003). *And miles to go . . .: State SLD requirements and authoritative recommendations.* {Electronic version} Nashville, TN: National Research Center on Learning Disabilities. Retrieved on July 21, 2005, from Vanderbilt University, National Research Center on Learning Disabilities Web site: http://www.nrcld.org/research/states

Reschly, D. J., & Gresham, F. M. (2006, April). *Implementation fidelity of SLD identification procedures.* Presentation at the National SEA Conference on SLD Determination: Integrating RTI within the SLD Determination Process, Kansas City, MO. Retrieved July 12, 2006, from http://www.nrcld.org/sea/presentations_worksheets/fidelity/Reschly.pdf

Sadler, C. (2002, October). *Building capacity in school-wide PBS.* Conference conducted at the Schoolwide Positive Behavior Support: An Implementer's Forum on Systems Change, Naperville, IL.

Shaywitz, S. (2004). *Overcoming dyslexia: A new and complete science-based program for reading problems at any level.* New York: Alfred A. Knopf.

Shinn, M. (1988). Development of curriculum-based local norms for use in special education decision-making. *School Psychology Review, 17*(1), 61–80.

Slonski-Fowler, K., & Truscott, S. D. (2004). General education teachers' perceptions of the prereferral intervention team process. *Journal of Educational and Psychological Consultation, 15*(1), 1–39.

Stanovich, K. (2005). The future of a mistake: Will discrepancy measurement continue to make the learning disabilities field a pseudoscience? *Learning Disability Quarterly, 28,* 103–105.

Steubing, K. K., Fletcher, J. M., LeDoux, J. M., Lyon, G. R., Shaywitz, S. E., & Shaywitz, B. A. (2002). Validity of IQ-discrepancy classification of learning disabilities: A meta-analysis. *American Educational Research Journal, 39*(2), 469–518.

Swanson, H. L. (1999a). Instructional components that predict treatment outcomes for students with learning disabilities: Support for a combined strategy and direct instruction model. *Learning Disability Research & Practice, 14*(3), 129–140.

Swanson, H. L. (1999b). What develops in working memory? A live span perspective. *Developmental Psychology, 35,* 986–1000.

Telzrow, C. F., McNamara, K., & Hollinger, C. L. (2000). Fidelity of problem-solving implementation and relationship to student performance. *School Psychology Review, 29,* 443–461.

Tilly III, W. D., Grimes, J., & Reschly, D. (1993, September–December). Special education system reform: The Iowa story. Communiqué, 22, 1–4.

Tomlinson, C. A. (1999). *The differentiated classroom: Responding to the needs of all learners.* Upper Saddle River, NJ: Pearson.

Torgesen, J. K. (2002). Empirical and theoretical support for direct diagnosis of learning disabilities by assessment of intrinsic processing weaknesses. In R. Bradley, L. Danielson, & D. P. Hallahan (Eds.), *Identification of learning disabilities: Research to practice.* Mahwah, NJ: Lawrence Erlbaum Associates.

U.S. Office of Education. (1999). Assistance to states for the education of children with disabilities and the early intervention program for infants and toddlers with disabilities. *Federal Register, 64*(48), 12505–12554.

Vaughn, S. (2002). Using response to treatment for identifying students with learning disabilities. In R. Bradley, L. Danielson, & D. P. Hallahan (Eds.), *Identification of learning disabilities: Research to practice.* Mahwah, NJ: Lawrence Erlbaum Associates.

Vaughn, S. (2003, December). *How many tiers are needed for response to intervention to achieve acceptable prevention outcomes?* Paper presented at the NRCLD Response to Intervention Symposium, Kansas City, MO. Retrieved March 15, 2006, from http://www.nrcld.org/symposium 2003/vaughn/index.html

Vaughn, S. & Fuchs, L. (2003). Redefining learning disabilities as inadequate response to intervention: The promise and potential problems. Learning Disabilities: Research and Practice, l8(3), 137–146.

Vaughn, S., Hughes, M. T., Schumm J. S., & Klingner, J. (1998). A collaborative effort to enhance reading and writing instruction in inclusion classrooms. *Learning Disability Quarterly, 21*(1), 57–74.

Vaughn, S., & Linan-Thompson, S. (2003). What is special about special education for students with learning disabilities? *The Journal of Special Education, 37*(3), 140–147.

Glossary

Accommodation—Any change made to instruction and/or assessment that does not change the expectations for performance or change the construct that is being measured respectively

Benchmark Tests—Short assessments (two to three minutes) given at the beginning, middle, and end of year to establish baseline achievement data and progress

Core Academic Subjects—English; language arts; reading; mathematics; science; the arts, including music and visual arts; social studies, which includes civics, government, economics, history, and geography; and modern and classical languages, except the modern and classical Native American languages and cultures of New Mexico tribes or pueblos

Curriculum-Based Measures (CBMs)—Direct assessments of student skills administered in standardized manner that are aligned to state content standards and benchmarks; student level results are typically graphed and compared to classroom peers to determine the student's level of progress

Duration—The length of time over which a child receives an intervention (e.g., fifteen weeks)

Early Intervening Services (EIS)—Refers to a broad application of scientifically based prevention and support services for students who are not identified as needing special education programs or service but who need additional academic and behavioral support to succeed in the general education classroom

Fidelity—Refers to the intensity and accuracy with which instruction and intervention are implemented

Fidelity of Implementation—The delivery of content and instructional strategies in the way in which they were designed and intended to be delivered: accurately and consistently; although interventions are aimed at learners, fidelity measures focus on the individuals who provide the instruction

Fidelity of Treatment—Implementing a program, system, or intervention exactly as designed so that it is aligned with research and ensures the largest possible positive outcome

Formative Assessment—A form of assessment intended to give students immediate feedback on their learning progress and to provide teachers with data regarding both what skills students have mastered and what skills are their areas of difficulty; it is used exclusively to drive appropriate instructional changes to meet individual student needs

Frequency—The number of times a child receives an intervention in a given time frame (e.g., daily, twice weekly)

Intensity—The length of time during which a child receives an intervention (e.g., thirty minutes)

Intervention—Instructional strategies and curricular components used to enhance student learning

Multitiered Service-Delivery Model or Tiered Service-Delivery Model—Provides tiers of increasingly intense interventions directed at more specific deficits and at smaller segments of the population

National Research Center on Learning Disabilities (NRCLD)—A joint project of researchers at Vanderbilt University and the University of Kansas with funding provided by the U.S. Department of Education, Office of Special Education Programs; NRCLD is part of a federal effort to find improved, research-based ways of identifying students with learning disabilities

Office of Special Education Programs (OSEP)—The Office of Special Education Programs is a federal program of the U.S. Department of Education dedicated to improving results for infants, toddlers, children, and youth with disabilities ages birth through twenty-one by providing leadership and financial support to assist states and local districts

Parent Involvement—The consistent, organized, and meaningful two-way communication between school staff and parents with regard to student progress and related school activities

Positive Behavioral Support (PBS) or **Positive Behavioral Interventions and Support (PBIS)**—A multicomponent approach to respectfully changing behavior while enhancing capabilities, opportunities, and quality of life

Progress Monitoring—A set of assessment procedures for determining the extent to which students are benefiting from classroom instruction

Research-Based (Activities, Practices, Instruction, Intervention, or Treatment)—Interventions or treatment approaches that have been scientifically demonstrated to be effective, regardless of the discipline that developed them

Research-Based Interventions—Instructional strategies and curricular components used to enhance student learning; the effectiveness of these interventions is backed by experimental design studies that (a) have been applied to a large study sample, (b) show a direct correlation between the intervention and student progress, and (c) have been reported in peer-reviewed journals

Response to Intervention—A system used at each school to screen, assess, identify, plan for, and provide interventions to *any* student at risk of school failure due to academic or behavior needs; it is an assessment and intervention process for systematically monitoring student progress and making decisions about the need for instructional modifications or increasingly intensified services using progress monitoring data

Schoolwide Screening—(also known as Universal Screening); an assessment characterized as a quick, low cost, repeatable test of age-appropriate critical skills (e.g., identifying letters of the alphabet or reading a list of high-frequency words) or behaviors (e.g., tardiness or discipline reports); measures are not too complicated and can be administered by someone with a minimal amount of training

Scientific, Research-Based—Research that involves the application of rigorous, systematic, and objective procedures to obtain reliable and valid knowledge relevant to education activities and programs

Scientifically Based (Activities, Practices, Instruction, Intervention, or Treatment)—Interventions or treatment approaches that have been scientifically demonstrated by research to be effective; under the No Child Left Behind Act of 2001, scientifically based research is defined as "research that involves the application of rigorous, systematic, and objective procedures to obtain reliable and valid knowledge relevant to education activities and programs"

Specific Learning Disability (SLD)—Specific learning disability (SLD) is one of the categorical conditions considered important for providing legal protections and entitlements; under IDEA 2004, SLD is defined as "a disorder of one or more of the basic psychological processes involved in understanding or using language, spoken or written, which disorder may manifest itself in [the] imperfect ability to listen, think, speak, read, write, spell, or do mathematical calculations. Such term includes such conditions as perceptual disabilities, brain injury, minimal brain dysfunction, dyslexia, and developmental aphasia. Such term does not include a learning problem that is primarily the result of visual, hearing, or motor disabilities, of mental retardation, of emotional disturbance, or of environmental, cultural, or economic disadvantage."

Tiered Service Delivery or Multitiered Service Delivery—Provides tiers of increasingly intense interventions directed at more specific deficits and at smaller segments of the population

Universal Screening—*See Schoolwide Screening*

Index

CORWIN PRESS

The Corwin Press logo—a raven striding across an open book—represents the union of courage and learning. Corwin Press is committed to improving education for all learners by publishing books and other professional development resources for those serving the field of PreK–12 education. By providing practical, hands-on materials, Corwin Press continues to carry out the promise of its motto: **"Helping Educators Do Their Work Better."**